TAKING

TAKING OVER

How to cope with your elderly parents

Avril Rodway

COLUMBUS BOOKS
LONDON

Acknowledgement: the quotation on page 22 from
Cider with Rosie by Laurie Lee is reproduced by
permission of the Hogarth Press

First published in Great Britain in 1987 by
Columbus Books Limited
19-23 Ludgate Hill, London EC4M 7PD

Phototypeset by Falcon Graphic Art Ltd
Wallington, Surrey
Printed and bound by
The Guernsey Press, Guernsey, Channel Islands

British Library Cataloguing in Publication Data
Rodway, Avril
   Taking over: how to cope with your elderly
   parents.
   1. Aged——Care and hygiene——Great Britain
   I. Title
   362.6'0941   HV1481.G52

ISBN 0 86287 252 9

Contents

Introduction

There is no easy answer to the problem of what happens to our parents when they grow old. Virtually everyone is now living longer, thanks to constantly improving medical care and higher standards of living. In the past thirty years the number of people over 65 has trebled, and the number living to over 85 has increased tenfold. By the year 2006, according to a British Medical Association report, there will be more than four million people over 75 in Britain, and more than one million over 85.

Many of these elderly people will not consider themselves as 'old' in the sense that they cannot cope, and will continue fit and active. A woman friend of mine aged 71 does all her own gardening, lays concrete paths, has quarry-tiled a garden room and will tackle almost anything, despite occasional attacks of angina. 'If I feel very tired, I just finish for the day and put my feet up,' she says. 'I'm fine next morning.' She also looks after her house and husband, who is equally fit, older than she is and does all the maintenance on his boat, which is his hobby. But 12 per cent of elderly people cannot even walk down the street without help, let alone go shopping, to the doctor or to collect their pensions. About 700,000 are unable to cook their own meals, 800,000 cannot wash or bath themselves and 200,000 find it difficult even to make a cup of tea.

According to the BMA, 'There is evidence that services are already inadequate and will become more and more inadequate unless greater resources are provided'.

This leaves a heavy burden of responsibility with families (and it is estimated that a family needs over £2,500 a year to care for an elderly relative) and with women in particular. One woman in eight is currently looking after a handicapped or elderly person; many of these women have children, and a significant proportion

7

have had to give up work, or at least take time off, in order to do so.

When talking to these 'carers' it soon becomes clear that although there are problems which are common to most such situations there are also very great differences. Much is accounted for by personality, attitudes, the amount of help available in the area, and so on. There are old people who are *too* independent and cause worry by not accepting enough help; there are families in which the old are neither valued nor aided and old people for whom the bitter remark 'No one wants you when you're old' is fully justified; there are carers who are selfless and devoted and who give up careers and prospects of marriage to devote themselves with cheerfulness and love to their elderly parents; there are selfish old people who let them do it. The variations are endless.

However, not all is gloom. Against one true account of a carer's hair turning white during the first two months of coping with a particularly difficult and exacting mother in her home, there are others of families deeply saddened by the death of a beloved grandparent who has lived with them for years as a member of the household.

Just as sharing the problems can be helpful when bringing up children, so knowing about other people's experiences in caring for an old person can also help. As far as possible, it is important to try to recognize an impending problem and plan to be able to deal with it. Assess the character of the person or people who may need to be looked after and, if possible, start preparing them, too. Do not forget that they also will have problems, which can either be physical, psychological or financial – or a combination of all three. It is vital to assess your own situation, too, what you can cope with, what the rest of your family can cope with, and what you can't. This book will, we hope, help you as a carer, or potential carer, with examples of other people's experiences, pointers to aid of various kinds, both voluntary and official, practical advice and information.

One of the saddest things about taking on the care or overseeing of an elderly person is that, unlike bringing a baby into the world and looking after it, the expectation has to be that things will get worse rather than better.

Carers have to be aware of changes and signs of physical or mental deterioration in their charges, know when to seek medical help and what aids, both financial and practical, are available. It takes a great deal of time and application to fill in forms, write to organizations and get as much as you and the old person are entitled to, as James found (see page 26). It also requires a great deal of tact and sympathy on your part when you are talking to a parent who may, after all, be very well aware of everything that is going on, the time you are spending and the deterioration in his or her own condition. Role reversal of this kind will, in all probability, be equally difficult for both of you.

An analysis of how the problems of ageing are coped with in different countries in the world would make fascinating reading. Our own impressions tend to be hazy. We probably feel, for example, that in countries such as India the extended family lives in the same village and all the old people are absorbed and looked after by younger members of their family, just as all the children there are used to being cared for by aunts and uncles as well as by their own parents. It is easy to forget that there the proportion of people living to old age is very much smaller than in the West, where advances in medicine, nutrition and hygiene standards all contribute to people surviving much longer. And what happens in America? Do most of their old people really go and live in versions of Sun City, with all the ladies keeping up their exercises and having blue rinses, and all the men playing bowls in panama hats in perpetual sunshine? Does every Italian family boast its ageless grandmother, dressed in rusty black, or its philosopher of an old grandfather, sitting forever under the olive trees and thinking about life?

In Britain, we seem to have our usual pattern of compromise. Most families want and try to care for their old people; if these elderly people need help, practical or financial, there are ways and means of obtaining it, though some of the forms may be so complicated that even the most well-meaning social worker may sometimes have difficulty in advising how they should be completed. However, some anomalies are being removed. The case of Mrs Jacqueline Drake recently came before the

European Court, which ruled that she and all married women (or women co-habiting as wives) who have to give up work and stay at home to look after someone elderly or handicapped are now entitled to the Invalid Care Allowance. Previously only men or single women could get it (they will of course continue to receive this allowance). This ruling will affect about 76,000 married women – certainly a step in the right direction. There will also be a change in the rules which will mean that many women will pay less tax on the benefit.

Now is perhaps the time for some campaigning, not only to help old people this year or next, but to ensure that a population with a rapidly increasing proportion of old people has had the forethought to look after itself. In early 1986 old people were dying of cold-related illnesses because they were afraid to turn on the heating in their homes and thus push up their fuel bills. Many believed they could not get an allowance to help them, and in a good number of cases they were right, for although many local authorities did, in fact, say they would help with increased allowances, albeit at a late stage, some did not. This is a situation which should not, in our comparatively affluent society, be allowed to exist. We do not appear to have benefited from cheaper oil, gas or electricity as some other European countries (France springs to mind) have done, and coal is certainly no longer cheap, nor is it practicable for many old people to use it.

Surely, too, the tax laws should be simplified so that it is not so difficult to work out, for instance, what amount of money an elderly person may earn before tax, or how much that tax will be?

Happily the problems of the elderly and the people who care for them seem to be increasingly in the news, so perhaps we are at last waking up to the fact that much more needs to be done. Let me quote just two examples, multiplied many times throughout the British Isles, as heartening examples of concern for carers.

The local centre for adult and continuing education in Norwich included in its 1985–6 prospectus a course called 'Caring for Older People' for just £6 for six two-hour weekly sessions, conducted by an SRN. The prospectus describes the course as being 'aimed at helping people care for older people whether they are relatives, friends, voluntary workers or helpers in residential homes. [It] discusses the broad issues of growing old in society today and some of the ways the carers can help the old maintain their independence.' Practical solutions to some nursing and medical problems were also offered, with lectures, discussions and workshops. A weekend course entitled 'Caring for the Old at Home' was also made available.

The second example is the splendid Lewisham (South London) Carers Project, which aims to 'look at the situation of carers in the Borough and to make recommendations regarding services to the Council and the Health Authorities'. The organizers set out to support informal carers (defined as 'people whose lives are restricted because they are looking after someone at home who is elderly, disabled, sick or frail – many of them being elderly or in poor health themselves') first by identifying their needs – for better transport, more respite care, improved co-ordination of services, more free time, more information about available resources, etc. – and by looking at the problems carers face. Some of these include psychological strain: carers rarely get a break from their 24-hour-a-day responsibility; physical strain; social isolation; lack of recognition by some professionals such as doctors and social workers; financial hardship; lack of practical support (home-based services are in short supply and priority is often given to those who live alone and who do not have a relative to help them); added disadvantages for women and for black carers. This particular council 'acknowledges the importance of supporting carers, and some services are provided with this aim in mind. But although quite generous when compared with many other areas, local services cannot provide enough help for most carers. The current financial difficulties faced by the Borough and by the health authority in particular raise doubts about the maintenance of services at their present level. It is therefore even more important that the needs of carers are recognized and budgeted for.' Much has already been done and such awareness of the problems of carers and desire to provide support and help in so many different ways is most encouraging. Many people caring for elderly relatives in the area have said how very helpful and supportive the local services have been.

As far as older people themselves are concerned, those over retirement age have often lost their economic 'clout'; they are no longer working and paying taxes. But let us not forget that they have done both for a large proportion of their lives and are entitled to all the benefits the state can offer and some that it should be offering. After all, it is our parents we are talking about . . . Next it will be us . . . then our children and our grandchildren . . .

RUTH

'Our "taking over" happened,' Ruth recalled, 'over a very long period, and at different times there were different difficulties and different positive features.

'When we had been married for a couple of years, my husband suggested that instead of living in rented accommodation we should combine to find a house to share with my parents which would be big enough for both families. They were already elderly, my father over 70 and ill with cancer, and my mother, although only in her sixties, disabled to some extent with rheumatism, so such an arrangement did make sense.

'Eventually, after some searching, we found a large house, which we bought very quickly and in which we lived for seven years. Here our first two children were born. It worked very well indeed at that stage as there was someone to leave the children with while I popped out to the shops, although my parents couldn't really cope with them for longer than an hour or so. We each had our separate kitchen and as we were all easy-going the arrangement proved a good one. This was out of London; at the end of the seven years it became necessary to move back and we went through a pretty chaotic time searching for accommodation for four adults, two children, a baby on the way and three dogs!

'After a short period in rented accommodation, with my parents staying elsewhere during the moves, which were shambolic, we at last found a house in South London, again with two kitchens. My father died nine months after this move, and after that I completely took over providing my

mother's meals, though she still liked to make cakes occasionally and do odd jobs like feeding the dogs or peeling vegetables.

'The difficulties became more complicated, as my mother had never spent a night alone throughout her life, and at her age (by now over 70) couldn't be expected to start. Luckily there was an old friend of the family who used to come over for a few days once a month, do some cleaning and gran-sit. It worked well as it gave us periods of resident babysitting and enabled us to go out as a family for the day, which wasn't possible if it meant leaving my mother alone. It was rather exhausting fitting in all our social life once a month into a few days, but on the whole we adapted and it worked well.

'My mother had acute attacks of rheumatism which put her into bed for some weeks – I felt her recovery was governed by her mood at the moment. I remember being pregnant, having two children to be fetched and carried from school, on foot as we had no car, plus a small child at home, and toiling up and down stairs with meals for my mother, who was showing no signs of getting better. I am sure she was very annoyed with me for having another child. When I told her that she would have to go away for the period of the confinement as Jon would not be able to cope with her as well as me and the children, she sat up in bed and said, "I'll be all right". And so she was, and eventually in her turn brought me the occasional cup of tea when I was in bed!

'Our last move was to our present house, where we have been ever since. This stage was happy and reasonably convenient. The children adored having a gran around. Her room was the quiet room and they liked joining her for a story or game of cards. She had the patience and time to help with reading, taught them to knit, gave wise counsel when there were difficulties and it was good to have someone to leave the baby with when I took the others to school in bad weather. Gran-sitting fitted in with babysitting. She was a very self-effacing person and did not intrude at all when we had visitors. It gave a great sense of security to the children to have Gran always in her room ready to listen and advise.

'Even when she became more and more dependent on me, especially as the children grew bigger and I wanted to be out more, it was the situation and not the person that irked me. But it did become increasingly difficult. I wanted to take up

13

*my own life to some extent. I had earlier started doing
voluntary social work and would dearly have liked to train
properly when my youngest started school, but I had ten more
years of my mother's increasing dependence on me.*

'My husband did not resent it, but as he had a practice of his
own he had an interest which took him out of the house a
great deal. He worked at home, and if I left food ready he
would give my mother her lunch if I wanted to be out for the
day. I had a cleaning woman two mornings a week who
would, if necessary, come late and stay over the lunch period
if he was out. It did enable me to start working – one morning
a week! The abiding memory of this long time is never doing
anything without having made elaborate arrangements and
always having a nagging anxiety that the arrangements might
go wrong . . . and always, always feeling I must hurry back.
Luckily Mother had always gone away to her much younger
brother for two holidays a year, and to my brother for one or
two visits. This enabled us to go on holiday and have some
time when we could all go out without any contriving on my
part, either all together or our separate ways. Without this
untrammelled time I feel I would not have survived. Holidays
were bliss, even all squashed in a caravan. I didn't have to plot
and plan.*

'This lasted until my mother was ninety, and these were
years during which she became increasingly dependent upon
me, whereas I felt an ever-greater sense of frustration as I
wanted to be off doing things. After her ninetieth birthday she
deteriorated rapidly. She only got up twice after it: once the
day after, in November, and once on Christmas Day.
Obviously there had been a steady deterioration before this,
but after her birthday she really made no more effort.*

'It was just a question of getting her to sit out in her chair in
her bedroom; increasing deafness made listening to the radio
impossible whereas she had kept up with what was happening
very well through years of being confined to the house.
Increasing blindness made it impossible for her to read. Her
mind began to wander; she slept most of the time or talked in a
rambling way to long-dead relatives. By this time it would
have been impossible to leave her without someone in the
house and I always seemed to be trying to contrive that
someone would prefer to stay at home.*

'The last ten months of her life were extremely difficult. She*

*became less and less responsive, very difficult over food and in
the end very disturbed. She would call out in the night that she
had fallen out of bed. Sometimes she had, sometimes she just
thought she had. I got her along to the lavatory in the
morning; she sometimes fell there and would always try and
clean herself with her fingers, so I would have to try to clean
her hands before getting her back to her room. By the time we
had finished her morning washing and toilet I was pretty
distraught myself.*

'*I was anxious that the children's happy memories of their
grandmother would not be clouded by her rather unattractive
condition and tried to cope mostly by myself, though they
were very helpful and my cleaner was also most supportive
and understanding. In May my mother went as usual to her
brother, but had to be taken by private [St John's] ambulance.
As the summer approached, my sister-in-law suggested asking
for a holiday admission [to hospital]. This was arranged, the
local council being very generous at that time. It was for two
clear weeks, with a couple of days either end to cope with
your own arrangements. She deteriorated rapidly in hospital,
had a fall and cut her head, and the nursing staff were
surprised that I had been able to cope. She went from hospital
to my brother's for a further two weeks, which gave me a good
break, but she had to be sedated a great deal while she was
there. There were a further two or three weeks of her at home,
which were exhausting, and then the hospital offered to take
her in.*

'*I knew it would finish her and I felt very guilty. But the
quality of her life was so low I did not feel it in any way
balanced the destruction of me and therefore my family. And
any delay made another fall likely and fractures a possibility.
She refused to go when the ambulance came, so we had to
arrange for it to come back the next day when the doctor was
in attendance.*

'*I could not bring myself to visit her as her condition was so
distressing and I felt guilty, but when relatives or friends
went, she begged them to take her out. After two weeks I went
to see her; her mind had suddenly cleared and she apologized
for being such a nuisance, and was her old courteous self. I
started planning my life to include a daily visit to the hospital,
but she developed pneumonia and died within three days.*'

Ruth also told me that in the family's last home, the local

GP had not been very helpful at first and only came when there was an acute need, such as a chest infection. But she did manage to convince him that her mother would benefit from a regular visit and he then came every four or six weeks and cheered her by his visits. He suggested arranging for her to be registered as partially sighted as he said it might be useful when and if she needed more care. And he arranged for a nursing auxiliary to come and give her a blanket bath occasionally. However, Ruth had the impression that any help was very difficult to come by and as she could cope she did not ask for more, so she did not really know if any more was available. The doctor did not offer holiday relief, but readily organized it when Ruth asked for it, and when she said she could not cope any longer, he acted swiftly. Ruth's only experience of voluntary helpers was the St John's Ambulance people.

Ruth felt herself lucky to have a family to back her up and to have help from outside members of the family. She now also realizes how fortunate she was to be within the area of a local authority which gives good relief services for carers; other authorities, she has heard, are not nearly so good. It is vital, she says, for carers to have breaks and to feel that there is help available, and if this cannot be supplied by the rest of the extended family it must be supplied officially, if only to prevent a complete breakdown. The alternative, in that event, would be that the state would have to care for two people or more, instead of partially caring for one. Ruth herself did not get much help, but did not need it most of the time; when help was needed it was supplied very rapidly. She was appalled by the stories she heard of other people coping for years on their own, and thinks she was one of the lucky ones.

Ruth ended her story on a humorous note. It seems that at the end her mother was unable to get out of bed without help – except that sometimes she managed in the middle of the night to get at the bottle of port which was kept in her room for a nightcap!

CHAPTER 1

How old is 'old'?

Mrs Florence Pritchard, aged 98, has decided not to seek re-election in the forthcoming council elections at Bewdley, Hereford and Worcester, after more than 50 years' public service. She is believed to be the country's longest-serving councillor.

Report in The Times

It may be a cliché, but there's quite a lot in the well-known saying 'You're only as old as you feel'.

Good health, stimulating company, interests, the ability to do things for other people, an active mind – all these can help to keep people who are no longer young in years young in outlook, active and fit. Nell's mother, now nearly 81, is still taking round meals-on-wheels to the 'old people', as she puts it. 'Can't afford to be ill,' she says. 'We haven't enough volunteers who can drive.' This may be an exceptional case, but one suspects not – there are many people over 60 who are caring for a husband or wife, or even a parent, whose disability makes him or her in need of looking after to some degree or other. And many, like Nell's mother, are doing voluntary jobs.

So 'old' need not necessarily mean 'infirm', and though, for the sake of convenience, I am writing primarily for readers who are looking after their elderly parents or parents-in-law, older readers in a similar situation may require just the same help and advice.

Often the pattern of life seems set in a comfortable routine. Granny and Grandpa are living in their retirement home, visited by their children and their children's husbands and wives, and enjoying seeing their grandchildren arrive and grow up. They do not feel particularly old; they enjoy good health, though they are aware that they have to take life more easily and that they have not the energy and resilience they once enjoyed. Various

17

events touch them, such as the death of friends and relatives of the same generation, and they may become aware that illness or disability is increasingly affecting people they know.

Changes may take place very gradually in their circumstances. They themselves may not be aware that these are manifestations of old age, although their visiting sons and daughters, who do not see them often, may be. Perhaps a bad winter, when one or other has 'flu and makes a slow recovery, or has a cold that hangs on and on or is followed by bronchitis, or has a fall and never quite gets better from it, will underline the fact that old age, as shown in the need for increased care, is creeping on.

On the other hand, the change may be sudden. Jane's mother, at the age of 65, had shingles badly in the summer. It left her feeling very low and unlike her usual self. She then started to get pains in the chest, associated with bad headaches, and to suffer badly from nightmares. However, a specialist could find nothing specific wrong with her and after a thorough check-up in November, he pronounced her fit, as far as he was concerned. At Christmas she was still under the weather and decided that she and Jane's father had better not make the 200-mile journey to spend the holiday with their daughter. She suggested that Jane and her young family came to visit them early in spring instead, during the better weather. The blow fell on Boxing Day when Jane's mother died with tragic suddenness from a coronary occlusion. The whole network of family relationships was disrupted and Jane's father, at the age of 69, rapidly became a dependent old man, no longer an active half of a long-married, happy couple.

Jane was an only child, and the worry of caring for her father was naturally her responsibility, but it very often happens in families that one member seems to shoulder most of the work and worry of caring for a frail or disabled relative. In some cases this is natural and accepted – Jane's father had done everything for his wife during the illnesses that led up to her death, and would not have had it otherwise. But where help is not forthcoming from members of the family who the main carer feels should be involved, resentment will fester.

Occasionally the unexpected happens. When Anna's mother died, Anna, who was very fond of him, gladly offered her 76-year-old father a home with her and was pleased at the prospect of his company. When after a year he announced that he had something important to tell her, her first thought was that he had had a bad report from the doctor about his health. However, the news he had to tell was that he was getting married again, 'to a very bouncy woman,' said Anna, 'quite unlike my mother. I didn't really know how to take it.' Faced with such a situation, most offspring will experience some inner conflict as feelings of loyalty towards the dead parent rise to the surface. What you have to remember, as anyone over 60 will tell you, is that old people don't feel old inside! In fact, many people are sexually active well into old age, and this should be accepted without ridicule or disgust as a happy manifestation of continuing interest in life.

Even if your parent or parents are infirm, they may still be capable of making decisions and should be consulted at every stage about their continuing care and what is going to happen to them. Sometimes this can cause severe problems.

Jacqueline's mother was determined to stay in her own flat 'as long as I can make myself a cup of tea', as she put it. This put a great strain on Jacqueline and her sister, who were both working full time and had families, as their mother had to have all her meals prepared or taken in, all her washing done, and had to be constantly visited to make sure she was all right. She was not on the phone, which was an additional source of worry, and she was not well. Then came the problem. Jacqueline's sister became ill herself, so ill that she could no longer help out with her mother, and all the burden fell entirely on Jacqueline. (There were also two brothers, but they lived some distance away and to a great extent had opted out.) Jacqueline had to call in before going to work, dash over at lunchtime and attend to her mother in the evening before getting her own family's meals.

At last her mother had a fall. She had got out of bed in the morning and was bending down to switch off her electric blanket when she lost her balance and tumbled over into the corner. Jacqueline found her there when she called in an hour later and got her straight to hospital. At last her mother agreed to go into the local sheltered flats for a trial period to see how she liked it – but Jacqueline told me with tears in her eyes that now her mother was back home and had managed to dress herself for the first time, she was afraid she would not agree even to the trial.

'She now takes things I say to her amiss – I chat to her as I would to my friends at work and she says, "You shouldn't talk to me like that, Jacqueline." I'm afraid that if she goes to the flats, one of the staff will say something she doesn't like and she won't agree to stay there. I've told her she can come to any of us at weekends – I've got my brothers to agree, too – and I don't work on Thursdays, so I could take her out then. One of the hardest things is to keep what's going on from my sister – she would feel awful that she isn't doing her bit for our mother. We're both so fond of her, you see.'

This difficult situation is typical, when the frail elderly person feels independent and wants to stay in her (or his) own home as long as possible but does not realize how dependent she is on the hard work and caring of her daughter or other relatives. It is a tricky situation and one in which it would probably be a good idea to call in the parent's doctor or a social worker who could advise in an impartial way, free from family emotional involvement.

When elderly people are mentally affected, this compounds the problems in many areas; in others, it can make them simpler. All the decisions will have to be made by the family, and they will have to be put over to the person concerned in the gentlest and most humane way possible. When a course of action is clear-cut – either that every source of outside help must be called into action if the parent is being looked after in a son's or daughter's home or by them in the elderly person's own home, or she must go into a suitable hospital or special residence for the elderly – then it can be easier than trying to persuade a reluctant, frail parent such as Jacqueline's that she needs 24-hour-a-day supervision.

Generally speaking, getting old is not a process people are very aware of in themselves. They will notice it more in others, but even when looking in the mirror, as we all know, we tend to cut out the things we don't want to see in our own appearance and concentrate on the good points: to quote from a poem written by an old lady who died in an old people's home in Leicester, 'You see an old woman, but you don't see me.' To ourselves we are always 25 inside. Personality changes are not so likely to take place as physical changes – a nervous person will tend to stay that way, a cantankerous one will probably always be cantankerous. However, there may be some mellowing and relaxation if circumstances surrounding the elderly person are calm, stable and well organized. If there are sudden, dramatic changes of personality, these may well point to an illness rather than to the effects of growing older.

The stresses on an older person will be different from those on younger ones. When we are battling to make our way in the world, carve out a career, make a go of our marriage, raise our families, cope with redundancy, etc., we have youth and resilience on our side, even if life is a struggle and money is short. Older people, with less energy, perhaps a disability or illness of some kind, may have to come to terms with the loss of a partner or members of the family, the feeling, now that their working life has come to an end, that their usefulness to society is over, that there will not be any improvement in their financial position, and that the standard of living, compared with previous years, may be very much lower – in fact that life is in decline, rather than likely to improve.

The ability to use distractions such as voluntary work, a hobby or interest, looking after grandchildren, reading with some goal in mind, can all help to combat the depression which can so easily and understandably attack the old. Sometimes a philosophical attitude will prevail, and a calm acceptance of a decline in physical powers and an ability to look on rather than joining in may manifest itself. However old people react to ageing, it is important to try to help in the appropriate way, either by accepting these reactions or offering sympathetic help or even just an ear that is willing to listen.

In the last year of his life, his wife having died three years previously, Jane's father talked to Jane a great deal about his experience of life, and told her that he would not be sorry when he eventually came to die. 'Not that I'd do anything to hasten it,' he said, 'but you come to find the world so very changed from what it was when you were young, you feel that the time has come to bow out and leave the running of things to younger people. And you're content just to get on with the small day-to-day things of life, so long as life is left to you.' As Laurie Lee wrote in *Cider with Rosie*:

So with the family gone, Mother lived as she wished, knowing she'd done what she could: happy to see us, content to be alone, sleeping, gardening, cutting out pictures, writing us letters about the birds, going for bus-rides, visiting friends, reading Ruskin or the lives of the saints. Slowly, snugly, she grew into her background, warm on her grassy bank, poking and peering among the flowery bushes, dishevelled and bright as they. Serenely unkempt were those final years, free from conflict, doubt or dismay, while she reverted gently to a rustic simplicity as a moss-rose reverts to a wild one . . . Then suddenly our absent father died . . . The mellow tranquillity she had latterly grown forsook her then forever. She became frail, simple-minded, and returned to her youth, to that girlhood which had never known him. She never mentioned him again, but spoke to shades, saw visions, and then she died.

Old age is just as much a piece of a person's life as childhood, youth and maturity, and the essential part, or spirit, of that person has a continuity even if the body is fragile, or the mind clouded. To show our parents or people we are caring for that they still matter as individuals and are still essentially the same people they always were is as important to our own characters as it is to them.

Perhaps what people fear most as they grow older is becoming mentally impaired. Physical frailty and disability they feel they can cope with so long as they still have their faculties, but we all dread 'senility'. Your parent may need reassurance that even in this event you would still think of her as a loved person, but one who, through no fault of her own, has become ill. (See Chapter 10.)

Coming to terms with the thought of one's eventual death and dissolution is hard for many younger people to contemplate, but old age often brings an acceptance which younger people find difficult to understand. This is not always so, of course. Angela's grandmother, who lived to be 85, was increasingly afraid of death as she grew older and suffered a variety of ailments, and her children found it very difficult to try to calm her. So both attitudes may be met with and need sympathetic and sensitive handling. If your parents are religious, it can be a great bonus at this time, and you will have back-up from priest or vicar and from members of their church. Pathetic delusions sometimes arise when elderly people are nearing the end of their lives. Joan's mother-in-law, the last time she visited her in the nursing home before her death, said to her, 'I don't feel so well, Joan. Can't you look up what's wrong with me in your red doctor's book and find a cure?' She had been so used to Joan always having the answer and a seemingly magical remedy at hand from a medical dictionary.

A question many people have to ask themselves is: at what point has ageing and/or disability advanced so far that we have to make a radical change in our lifestyle or manner of caring for our parent, either taking her into our home, getting more outside help for her, or persuading her to go into sheltered accommodation or an old people's home? Is she reasonably mobile, able to go out for a walk, do shopping, cope with buses and cross roads on her own, etc.? Or would it be desirable for her to have help with shopping, or someone to accompany her when she goes out? Indoors, can she cope with the everyday business of living – getting up and dressed without too much difficulty, going to the lavatory, washing and taking baths on her own, cooking her own food and feeding herself without help, cutting her own toenails, doing her washing and ironing, etc.? If you list the things she cannot do, or has difficulty in doing, you should be able to assess the level of help that is needed, either from yourself or from another carer, or from locally provided services.

One of the most difficult problems you may face is to get your parent to admit that help is needed; like Jacqueline's mother, to whom independence was so very important, your parent may need to be persuaded by a slight shock if he or she is reluctant to accept your arguments. Admitting that age has brought the need for more support is more difficult for some people than others. This individuality should constantly be borne in mind – just as all 'children' or 'teenagers' are not alike because of their common ages, neither can the 'elderly' or 'senior citizens' be lumped together as a single entity. Everyone is different, just as they have been throughout life, and many of the illnesses which well-meaning relatives put down to 'simple old age', are not necessarily so and may very well be able to be cured.

It is easy to give advice and suggest that if your elderly parent needs help or treatment she will be given it simply as a result of applying in the right quarter. This will depend on local resources, how you or she applies and who helps to progress the requests. It very often takes time and a lot of effort, as James found, to contact the right people, to write the correct letters and fill in forms properly. It may seem the last straw at the end of a busy working day to come home and try to sort out the problem of getting a home help or a telephone installed for your parent. It is, however, much better to write rather than telephone about any particular problem with which your parent needs aid. For one thing you can keep a copy of the letter, whereas the details of telephone conversations tend to get forgotten; and correspondence will enable the professionals or charities you are contacting to keep a file on your particular case for their reference.

Your attitude may be very important in getting the help you need for your parent. A patient, honest account of the problem, your involvement and how you are affected will be most likely to get you a sympathetic hearing and the help that is needed rather than making demands, adopting an aggressive attitude and expecting an immediate favourable response. You will find that organizations such as Age Concern or the local Citizens' Advice Bureau (CAB) can be valuable allies; so may people going into your parent's home, such as a social worker or home help, who can give you useful advice on how best to approach a department and office, and, almost more important, tell you whom to approach. If you have a complaint, on the other hand, you should *not* initially write a letter; instead, go and see the person involved if at all possible. He or she may have misunderstood your request, or may have good reasons for not being able to supply whatever is needed straight away.

What are the main needs of the elderly? Basically, of course, they are the same as for anyone, whatever one's age: security, both physical and financial, friendship and love, feeling useful and wanted, and being allowed to make as many personal decisions as possible, from minor ones (like choosing what food to have – after all, our parents have done it all their lives) to major ones such as where to live and what constitutes quality of life.

Unfortunately, compulsory retirement at 65 and 60 for women (now to be changed) can at one blow undermine the basic security people have enjoyed for many years (the government is however discussing plans to make the retirement age more flexible). Not only do the retired have to face the loss of colleagues and friends they saw regularly through their work, and probably to adapt to a much lower standard of living, but the pattern of their life is broken and their feeling of usefulness in society has gone, giving them a sense of lowered status. Particularly in men, retirement is often quickly followed by death as they fail to adapt to a different lifestyle. Much as they may have looked forward to more leisure and not being answerable to anyone but themselves, their sense of loss may be almost the equivalent of a bereavement. In recognition of this problem, there is now more activity to help people prepare for retirement. The Pre-Retirement Association, for example, which produces a magazine called *Choice*, has that aim (see Chapter 12).

In some countries, the experience and advice of the elderly are valued and old age has a respected place in society. In Britain, unfortunately, this is not generally the case, unless the individual is a member of certain of the professions. Judges and politicians, for example, can go on until a ripe old age. However, the idea of being useful to society in other ways than of being in paid employment gives satisfaction to very many people who have left work. This is why such bodies as the British Legion, W.I., the Lions, church organizations, etc. are so valuable – not simply for the good work they do for charities, but also for the good work they do for individuals over retirement age who, like Nell's mother, go on working tirelessly for them, fund-raising, visiting and taking over all manner of difficult jobs, not for financial gain but for the personal satisfaction of feeling useful and wanted, and working with other people for a common objective.

Very often it may seem to older people that the only way they can make a mark and be recognized as individuals is to be demanding and difficult, rejecting suggestions for a change of residence or for changes in their homes. These may be small decisions, but ones which show that they still have a voice which has to be listened to. So if a parent is being 'bolshie' about something which clearly needs to be done to make his or her home safer and pleasanter, it may be that your way of putting over the advantages of the change has been too dictatorial or insensitive, or that it is time to involve outside help.

JAMES

James was divorced, so the whole burden of caring for his old parents, aunt and mentally handicapped sister fell on him. This problem was compounded by the fact that he lived in London while the others were all in Devon, so any arrangements he made for them had to be organized at long range. He also had a full-time job and was very concerned for the welfare of the three children of his marriage, whom he saw very often. When his parents started to be a problem, his children were 16, 11 and 8 years old respectively.

He first noticed a deterioration in his parents when his father became partially blind and his mother started to suffer from reduced mobility. His first action was to persuade them to move to more suitable accommodation, a change he had to be responsible for organizing. His own reactions were first of all sadness and despair, then increasing frustration. His ex-wife and children rallied round, however, with offers of help as far as was practical in view of the distances involved.

One of the main effects the problem had on his life at first was the need for him to take time off, during working hours, since many visits had to include dealing with the DHSS, Health Centre, banks, etc. He felt continually tired, and suffered both physical and mental strain. But he felt no resentment except against the medical establishment, who seemed to be particularly obstructive in the area where his dependants lived.

When asked what mental and emotional effects the situation had on him personally, James described them as 'those of a waking nightmare'. His advice to other people in similar circumstances is, first, to make sure that any retirement move on the part of the elderly people is a wise one. Either the potential carer or the parents should live for a while or have a prolonged holiday in the chosen town, during which they ask about local medical facilities. Remember that a gentle slope for the car could become a heart-thumping grind for an elderly person on foot carrying shopping. Find out about buses, mini-cabs and retailers who will deliver. It will save endless problems if you, as carer, can gently insist on such research at retirement stage. Thereafter, and if the parents are not living in the carer's home or on his territory, make personal contact with all who can help – doctor, health visitor, W.I., Age Concern, etc. – and explain the actual or potential problems. Exchange address and phone numbers with them and make it abundantly clear that you are 'responsibly in charge'.

James also advises 'riding roughshod (with as much loving diplomacy as possible) over all attempts to resist innovations such as bedside emergency bells, walking frames, telephone extensions, safety gear for baths, the elimination of potentially lethal clutter such as slip mats (they are!), long, looping electrical leads, shelves holding items which can only be reached by standing on a stool, or whatever.

'I took the lock off the loo/bathroom door,' he said, 'and substituted a written notice on a piece of card, saying 'ENGAGED'. This could be turned over to its blank side when the lavatory was not occupied. I also encouraged the eating of convenience foods, which may seem strange nowadays when "healthy eating" is so fashionable and no one has a tin in sight. However, I went on the principle that it was better for my parents to get adequate nutrition in the form of frozen beef in gravy or a can of baked beans than for me to encourage elaborate cooking operations using fresh food, which they probably wouldn't have had either the strength or the desire to carry out.'

Another piece of advice James had to offer was: 'Don't assume all OAPs welcome a succession of friendly, helpful visitors; some, however hospitable, want privacy when they want it. Discourage all surprise visits from anyone, including family. Remember that to many elderly and infirm people, routine is their last dignity. Don't forget that dignity. Make sure (by whatever means) that your mother has the opportunity, even if she doesn't take it, of having her hair done. Make sure that your father is never unshaven; sometimes an electric shaver in someone else's hands can work wonders for the morale!

'*Dignity again. Bite your lip and block your nose. Their failure to be able to continue the personal hygiene routine they once took for granted is as much a source of indignity to them as it is offensive to others.*'

When asked about helpers, James was complimentary about the aid given by the social services to his parents. They were well-intentioned and helpful with walking frames, pincers for picking things up, etc. Less standard items, however, sometimes arrived too late. 'For example, a mini-ramp to enable my mother to overcome a step to the garden arrived long after she was capable of, or desirous of, getting into the garden. On the whole, though, no complaints. Meals-on-wheels were marvellous, the only gripe being that food was delivered in four-ton lots served on tea plates. Chips and/or instant mash with everything, but that isn't really a complaint about the service, which was excellent.

'However, the Health Centre and member doctors were dreadful! Appointments there very frequently resulted in a wait of up to three hours. House visits often came four days after the telephone calls. All the doctors had badly swollen wrists caused by pernicious prescription-writing and could therefore be pardoned for writing infinitely repeatable prescriptions. My parents had a fair-sized tea-tray completely covered with bottles of pills.

'There was also obstruction. It was clear that my father would never again be a well man, but also that quite probably his declining days could be made happier – physically and in terms of morale – by some form of treatment. I wanted a second opinion, and managed to find a private medic in a neighbouring town who was happy to visit provided he got a referral from the NHS GP. This I could not get. The Health Centre doctor flatly refused. In London this would not be a problem; in a relatively small (but widespread) rural community it proved an insuperable one.

'Bad diagnosis (or none) was another failing. When my father was hallucinating and frequently in deep lethargy, the Health Centre doctor visited him, took him into the hall and made him stagger up and down a few times with a walking frame. Turning to my mother, he said something like: "There, Mrs —, you must not let him go to sleep in his chair all day." Two weeks later, my father was dead of a massive coronary.

'As we all know, or suspect, big is not beautiful, although it may be lucrative. From an NHS standpoint, there was in the town where my parents lived no alternative to the giant Health Centre and its eight doctors. No one partner is going to contradict the findings of another. And if you don't like it, you can die. For dying, there is a nice, friendly (no sarcasm – true) cottage hospital where the elderly are sent "for a little rest". If they die at the first visit, then that's neat and tidy. If they don't, they come out again to the same old GP routine in the hope that they'll die at home.'

James's mother died shortly after her husband; then there was, as he put it, a 'repeat prescription'. My parents were both dead, leaving my mentally handicapped sister, aged 57, with my maternal aunt, aged 74, because of a deathbed promise between sisters. Despite all kinds of expensive outside help with cleaning, shopping, etc. this soon put my aunt into hospital. The local social services were called in and placed my sister in a loving, caring home (that of a private family, not an institution) where she was to be treated as a family member. My aunt came out of hospital too weak to boil an egg and my sister remained with the family. After my aunt's first nocturnal collapse, when she was too weak to reach the telephone, a private night nurse was installed from bed- to breakfast-time and a new phone and bedside bell were put in. I tried again to get a second medical opinion, with the same result as before. My aunt returned to hospital and died.

'By a pure and unpredictable accident, it was discovered that my sister's social worker (visiting the family fortnightly) hadn't been. My sister was in decline, had been mildly terrorized, was incontinent and twitching. She was removed to a private home after considerable vetting of the place, and now appears to be blossoming, fitter – and happier than for many a year.

'If this sounds like a condemnation of the social services as far as she was concerned, it is, though only in that particular

29

town. But it is fair to say that my sister's condition was spotted by someone in a short-stay home in the nearby town where she had been sent while the private minder was in hospital. They called me into a committee meeting and presented me with a well-written observational analysis of my sister during her stay there. So they're not all idiots – far from it.'

James certainly had some major problems on his hands, not just with one or two, but with no less than four dependent relatives. What would he advise others caring for elderly parents to do in the light of his experience?

'It's hard to be specific,' says James. 'It's really horses for courses. I was unable to have my dependants in my house for various reasons; other people have to. Attitudes and emotions have to vary, not for reasons of loyalty or lack of it, or love or responsibility, but for logistical and geographical reasons.

'Emotionally, I know of no solution other than biting the bullet, knowing that it can't last forever, and having a few friends who understand – without your having to subject them to long, boring accounts of your trials and tribulations. If the carer and his/her old folk are gregarious, then organize some tea-and-bun parties with the similarly afflicted and get in touch with all state and voluntary bodies that may be able to do something.

'Financially, do your homework (and it is work) and screw the state because it's been screwing us for you. Research the **Charities Digest**. Look for, but do not expect, financial help from relatives.

'As far as admin goes, get used to the fact that you'll have to write to organizations and that you must keep copies. Be prepared to receive telephone and written communications which will be gobbledegook if you haven't kept copies of what you wrote after research. In terms of state organizations, accept that the letter you wrote to Newcastle office may elicit a reply from Blackpool or Swansea. With all such departments and at all times, hit them very hard with a suède glove on which has been painted a smile. Never forget that the CABs can be very helpful, at no cost, if you're prepared to hang around a bit for your appointment. Remember that such things as sheltered accommodation are available "on the state", but not enough of them.'

Though it was obviously short on comic relief, James does

recall one gloriously memorable incident from the period: 'One morning after my aunt had been taken ill in the night, the cleaning lady couldn't get in and rang the doctor. A lady doctor appeared and decided to break in through a partially open window at the rear of the flat. Unfortunately she got stuck halfway and the local police nearly arrested her tweed-clad bum and kicking tights. Wish I'd been there!'

CHAPTER 2

Who 'takes over'?

Some people, discussing the need for helping parents as they grow older, disliked the term 'taking over'. As Libby remarked, when there was a joint decision that her mother-in-law should move into a flat closer at hand, 'I would not say that we have "taken over" my mother-in-law's life. She remains a very independent lady, living in her own flat.' And Sandra, whose mother had a sudden stroke and became semi-paralysed, remembers: 'I was terribly upset to see my mother, who was an independent lady running her own home, brought to these straits.'

In very many cases, carers not only do not want their parents to feel that they have taken over their lives, but do not in fact feel that they have done so. In other cases, however, where illness or incapacity is very great, the carer really *has* to take over in every area whether it is long-range or intimate physical care. In the past there have been difficulties in administering the individual's resources to the best advantage in the event of a parent becoming confused or losing his or her mental faculties. Now, with the introduction of a new Act providing for an Enduring Power of Attorney, this aspect of caring should become easier for many people with elderly dependent relatives (see Chapter 8).

Although the combinations of cared-for and carers are very wide-ranging, as you will see from the case histories in this book, it certainly seems that the role of carer usually falls to one family or individual. Recently the organization formed to help 'The Single Woman and Her Dependants' changed its name and widened its scope – but the earlier name certainly underlined the fact that there were very large numbers of single women acting as carers on their own.

Perhaps single women are more likely to agree to take on the role assigned to them by other members of their families or by society and feel that they must fulfil it. Very often the reason for 'sacrifice' is great conscientiousness and an underlying feeling of guilt: 'I owe it to her. After all, she did so much for me when I was young that I should be glad to help her and look after her in her declining years.' But of course, it is not often stated that there is genuine affection and love in many relationships between parent and child, even if the day-to-day strain of living together causes friction and arguments. Greta, who since she grew up had actively disliked her father (and he her) and had never had anything to do with him if she could help it, found herself in the position of being the only person to look after him in his old age (he was 87 when he came to live with her). Much to their surprise, their relationship developed into one of mutual respect and affection which both found extremely rewarding.

A similar thing happened to May (see her story, page 106). From dreading the day when her father moved in, she came, as she said, to like him as well as love him. Very often it is the woman in the family who is the main carer. If she is supported in the task, however, it can make an enormous difference. When she read what was written about her, May, who has been looking after an invalid husband and three small children as well as her old, blind father, said, 'I sound so smug! Is it possible just to say that really I was only able to do it because I was so loved and had such a marvellous marriage and home life? True, my husband didn't knock too many nails in, but he had a much more valuable gift – of giving and inspiring love. He never lost his temper and I suppose because he thought the sun shone out of me (and I of him) it made the atmosphere possible. That and a big house. If those hadn't been there, I know I would have been a nervous wreck. Bickering and bitterness are so utterly valueless and corroding.'

Many of the women carers interviewed remarked upon how immensely supportive their husbands or partners had been, though some also said that before they took the job on they had no idea how demanding looking after an elderly parent would be – nor how much strain it would put on their marriage and other relationships within the family, particularly those with older children. Trying to divide yourself up between a number of people, all competing for your attention, is never easy in a family, and one or two extra people, in the shape of a parent or parents, can add immeasurably to that difficulty.

In Sandra's case, though, it was her grown-up son who was her main support. When her mother first had a stroke he 'helped in every way. In the beginning, when she was a dead weight, I couldn't have managed without him. But we have always been a close family.'

For one person on his or her own, caring for a relative of course has its own problems: loneliness, the feeling that you, the carer, can never get away, the fear of being ill with no one to take over your role – all these can add up to a fearsome responsibility. Many carers are themselves elderly, and are looking after a husband or wife. Indeed, it is very often elderly people who are most reluctant to admit that they cannot cope any longer or are in desperate need of outside support. Pride will often not let them admit that their partner's mental condition has deteriorated or that physically they cannot do what is required in the way of housework, lifting or nursing.

The Association of Carers (address in Chapter 12) quotes some startling figures on caring, which are steadily increasing as the proportion of elderly people in the UK population grows. Over a million and a quarter people in Britain today are leading restricted lives because they are looking after a disabled or elderly relative; 100,000 carers have been doing this for ten years or more, and if just 1 per cent of those caring for an elderly relative were to give up, the health and social services budgets would have to increase immediately by 20 per cent. Those people caring for the elderly at home are saving statutory services £5.3 billion every year, and although the cost of a bed in a residential establishment is now between £140 and £500 a week, the maximum state attendance allowance, available only to the most severely disabled living at home, was, in 1985, £28.60 a week. Carers' ages range from as young as 4 to as old as 99 – many elderly people are looked after by relatives in their seventies and eighties. A survey quoted by the Association showed that over 60 per cent of carers are themselves in poor health and cannot easily seek treatment as there is no one to take over at home.

Some of the stories the Association cites are harrowing. 'I feel guilty for writing to you, but I nursed my mother until she died at the age of 89 after being in failing health for years. I am now nursing my husband, who is 75. I am 70 myself and he has been disabled for the last 15 years. The physical strain is great and I am worried about how long I can manage . . .' 'I am caring for my mother and father. My father has suffered a stroke and my mother suffers with myxoedema, which means she is an imbecile, unable to be left, unable to do anything herself. I cannot get the state Invalid Care Allowance because it is not paid to married women [a situation which is happily to be remedied in the near future]. I have received no visit from the social services since 1981.'

The problems of carers are many, one of them being the difficulty of gathering all the helpful information possible, for they are frequently as housebound as the person for whom they are caring. Membership of the Association brings with it the booklet mentioned earlier called *Help at Hand*, 'a signpost guide for carers'; it covers benefits, services and the emotional aspect of caring (see page 215).

The Association was founded in 1981 by a woman who is herself a carer with a starter grant from the Equal Opportunities Commission. When she needed to go into hospital for a serious operation no help was offered by the social services for her invalid husband and children other than the suggestion that the two children should be taken into care and her husband sent to a hospital miles away. This experience made her realize just how desperate was the need for a campaign to try to get better conditions and help for carers and to provide support and advice for people in need of it. (In her own case, she opted to have the operation under a local anaesthetic, came out of hospital the same day and immediately took up caring for the children and her husband again.)

The support the Association gives takes many forms. Letters from carers are answered on an individual basis, which often involves a great deal of research to make sure that each person gets the best and most relevant advice. In one year alone, the Association answered 22,000 such letters, and the numbers are growing. It helps in setting up local self-help and support groups so that individual carers may feel that they are not alone in their problems – a great morale-booster as well as a source of practical help. According to the Association's information leaflet, it had 60 such requests in hand at the time of writing. Each required at least two visits, a starter pack of information material for the group co-ordinator and follow-up support.

The Association claims that it has done more than any other organization to educate professionals in the needs of carers – but there is a lot more to be done in campaigning for increased resources both nationally and locally. Pressure on families to take on the care of their ill and elderly relatives is increasing as state resources diminish and the numbers of elderly increase. People are often made to feel guilty if they do not take over the responsibility of caring, however unsuitable their houses may be or however difficult their family circumstances. Geriatric hospitals are suffering cuts and private homes are very expensive, far beyond the reach of most families; moreover, there is often a great deal of unkind and uncalled-for criticism of someone who is 'putting her mother away' in a home.

Another organization which declares, 'We care for carers of the elderly' is the National Council for Carers and Their Elderly Dependants (formerly The National Council for the Single Woman and Her Dependants, mentioned earlier). It has been helping and advising carers for over twenty years and its booklet covers, for example, information sources and planning, with lists of useful supporters to contact; voluntary organizations; notes on tax and benefits; where to get aids and equipment; how to get a short-time break from caring; educating yourself on caring; and other useful information including details of the NCCED Pen Friends Club, which is particularly appreciated by carers who are virtually housebound or who are not able to have many personal contacts; a list of short-stay homes (suitable names will be given to enquirers who send details of the personal needs of the invalid requiring care); a short list of volunteers who are willing to live in the family home with an elderly or infirm person to enable the carer to have a holiday or rest (extra volunteers are, they say, always welcome), etc.

The Council has successfully campaigned for various legislative measures to help carers, and has been responsible for many worthwhile projects such as the Granny Sitting Service idea (see Laura's case history, page 192), the short-term relief network and the formation of over 50 branches and groups. As the Council says: 'Our work is about improving the quality of life of old, infirm and disabled people and their carers. We have helped hundreds of thousands such people. We do it well. Those we have helped have a better life.' For the Council's address, see Chapter 12.

Both these charitable organizations do excellent work for carers and are of course delighted to receive support in the form of fund-raising and/or subscriptions.

Perhaps you are reading this book because you are yourself are a carer, with the problems and hard work that this implies. Eventually we ourselves may be in the position of having to be cared for, and now is the time for lobbying, not only to ensure that help is forthcoming at this moment, to help us in caring, but for the future to help our children look after *us*. At least it might be possible to straighten out some of the ridiculous anomalies which come to light – such as the case of the carer who had to give up his job and take supplementary benefit in order to be on hand to help lift a weighty and completely incapacitated relative each morning. The benefit cost the state many times more than it would have cost to pay someone to do the necessary morning lifting.

The extraordinarily unfeeling attitude of some doctors towards carers was revealed in a recent newspaper report:

Sending old people to hospital *just to give holidays to their daughters or whoever looks after them at home* [my italics] can be a death sentence, say a group of London doctors. A survey conducted from Whittington Hospital, Highgate, found nine "holiday admissions" out of 69 died, a death rate of over 13% compared with under nine for genuinely ill old people. No one knows why these old people are so vulnerable when taken from their homes, says the doctors. But doctors, relatives and community workers were too quick to suggest a move to hospital. It should be discouraged.

Without holidays and breaks many carers would suffer complete breakdown themselves – and where would that leave us? Obviously there is a great need for care in the home, as well as for that funded by the state, but it must be recognized that some expenditure is necessary by government in order to avoid even heavier expenditure, and this includes funding for state-run organizations in the community that can help to lighten the burden of carers.

LIBBY

'My mother-in-law lived 22 miles away from us,' said Libby, 'and about two-and-a-half years ago she told us that she seemed to be growing frailer and was finding it difficult to cope. Naturally we were very worried, but as she is a very sensible woman and has all her faculties it has not been the major problem that it might have been.

'Tim and I responded by visiting more frequently, giving more practical help in the house and garden and doing all her shopping and washing. With her agreement, we began to investigate sheltered accommodation, nursing homes, etc., but these all proved unsatisfactory, so eventually we found a ground-floor flat with a good caretaker, within five minutes' reach of our own house. The change was accomplished easily as my mother-in-law appreciated the very real need she had to live nearer to us and yet to remain independent.

'It was a great relief to us as we were relieved of the stress of driving more than 40 miles across London every Saturday, and of a great deal of worry, too. We don't have to spend more time in helping her and we are able to see her for shorter periods but more frequently.

'I would say that we have not "taken over" my mother-in-law's life as she remains a very independent lady, living in her own flat. The people she is most dependent upon are the social services, who provide a home help to shop and clean for her when I am not able to. In fact, our local social services have been extremely helpful, although they took a few weeks to respond to our applications for help. We haven't needed to call upon any of the voluntary organizations as we are able to provide a lot of company, driving around, etc. I do think

something on the lines of home help but for gardening –
"garden help" – would be useful and enable elderly people to
remain in their own homes longer.

'I know we've been lucky. To people in our situation I only
have one word of advice – if you're moving a parent from a
house she may have lived in for 50 years, as Tim's mother had
done, to a smaller home, do be very, very firm or even quite
ruthless about possessions. Otherwise you may end up as we
have done, with a cellar bursting at the seams with carpets,
pictures, kitchen tools, garden tools, books – and even a gas
refrigerator!'

CHAPTER 3

Left alone

Apart from illness, infirmity or mental or physical deterioration, the widow- or widowerhood of a parent is probably a major factor in precipitating a change of lifestyle for an elderly person and his or her offspring. The first shock, doing all that has to be done to arrange a funeral, dealing with kind offers of help, answering letters of sympathy – all this makes for a period of great activity. It may seem like a good idea to try to sort out long-term arrangements at this time as well as seeing to the immediate necessities. A son or daughter may be tempted to say, right away, 'You must come and live with us' as much as the parent may be tempted to accept.

When Jane's mother died, very suddenly on Boxing Day in her own home (see Chapter 1), many miles away from where Jane lived, Jane had to rush down to Cornwall to support her father, leaving her husband in charge at home to look after their two tiny children. It seemed best to arrange the funeral as quickly as possible and to sort out her mother's clothes and possessions straight away, agonizing as she found it. But looking back she says:

I'm not sure I was right. I think both my father and I needed more time to come to terms with our grief. It seemed a bit like sweeping someone's whole life away under the carpet. My father kept weeping and insisting that I went into the bedroom to look at my mother, who was laid out at home, not in the undertaker's chapel of rest, and I had to do it for his sake, though it nearly finished me off. He obviously didn't feel as I did that there was no one there, my mother had left her body. To him that shell was a dear and vital part of her and all he had left. I couldn't wait for the funeral, awful as it was. He and I and two neighbours were the only mourners as there wasn't time for any other members of the family to arrange to come down from the North of England.

Jane took her father back with her to London for a

prolonged visit and this period of calm and change was a good thing for everyone.

His first subconscious reaction was a series of small illnesses, needing visits to the doctor and lots of fuss and attention, and, in fact, this was supportive to him. When he went back to his own house, Jane went with him – no one should have to return to an empty house alone in such circumstances. During the time Jane stayed with him, they worked out a routine for shopping and house-work and Jane had a quiet word with his kindly young neighbours and the doctor. Fortunately her father had always been very domesticated and had helped his wife a lot with the house, so from that point of view he was able to cope well and look after himself. Jane insisted that a telephone was installed, which her parents had felt able to do without when her mother was alive, and this proved invaluable. She rang him regularly and was able to check that he was well and managing all right.

It was decided that he would try and cope in his own home for a time, and that Jane and her family would come down at Easter and reassess the situation then. They had a long discussion and decided that it might be best if he sold his bungalow and found a flat which was easy to manage and near Jane, so that she could give him a hand and he could have company. In fact, he changed his mind at the last minute and went on living in his own home until the end of his life. For him, facing the upheaval of moving, the effort of making new friends and the sadness of leaving his familiar neighbourhood outweighed the advantages of being near his daughter, and ultimately the decision was his.

The practical problems for an elderly man left alone are likely to be different in some respects from those of a woman in the same circumstances. For him, physically coping with domestic matters may seem at first to be an insuperable problem – this may all have been his wife's province and she may have enjoyed fussing over her husband and doing everything for him. It may be possi-ble to arrange some domestic help, either privately or through the social services, and it would be a good idea if you, as carer, could make personal contact with the social services, a local charity or your father's GP: not only would this help with the practical problem of providing domestic help, but it would also ensure regular visits if he lives a long distance away from you. If you live near enough to pop in often to see him and help, it is important not to take over the running of his home for him as your mother did. Not only will you probably not have time, but it will help him to be more independent and give him things to do if you can show him how to help himself, what quantities of food he should be buying and how to keep the house clean – provided he is well, of course.

Obviously these problems will not be the same if an elderly married woman is left on her own, but in her case she may not have been used to coping with family finances, filling in official documents and forms, and all that side of life which her husband was used to regarding as his province. It is important to try to help her sort this out (see Chapter 8), so if you yourself find it difficult enlist the aid of a social worker, the Inland Revenue, Age Concern or a Citizens' Advice Bureau. Make sure she is receiving all the benefits and help to which she is entitled, and that her pension is sorted out and any extra benefits which are payable are in fact coming her way.

It may help to have a talk about money with her and work out a budget for one person rather than two, as suggested in Chapter 8. If she is remaining in her own home, of course, such bills as heating, rates, etc. will be at the same level, but her income will be less than it was when her husband was alive, so she may find it more of a struggle to manage. If there is a problem of this kind, seek official help. One of the major causes of anxiety among old people is money, and it is important to relieve the burden of this stress for your parent if at all possible. Encourage her to talk about it and suggest ways of helping. Writing down the budget will provide a reassuring framework within which she can work.

On a practical level, make sure that your mother can cope with the tasks your father may have done. If she has a coal fire, for example, is she strong enough to get the coal in and cope with clearing out the grate and removing the ash? It might be time to think about installing a different type of heating, if finances allow. Is the garden of a manageable size? Can she cut the grass (this often emerges as a major worry for old people left alone)? Perhaps some help could be arranged: sometimes voluntary organizations can supply someone to lend a hand from time to time, or there may be an elderly male neighbour who could come round and do a few gardening jobs for a small fee.

Take a look round the house from the safety point of view. If one person living alone has an accident, it could be far more serious than if a partner were on hand to report it or call the doctor. Your mother, particularly, may be worried about break-ins and burglaries, so make sure that secure locks are fitted (but not ones she will find unmanageable) and if possible fit a 'peep-hole' device on her front door so she will be able to see who is calling.

Another practical problem may be transport. Your father may have had a car, but your mother may never have learned to drive and particularly if she lives in an isolated village this may present difficulties. Fortunately neighbours are usually ready to rally round and help, perhaps with a weekly shopping trip to a nearby town, and there may be volunteer transport to luncheon clubs and meetings which can be taken advantage of.

Of course, you will resist any urge to move in and make a lot of changes without discussing matters with your parent first. She may oppose certain suggestions and you will have to accept her opposition, but you may find that she turns the ideas over in her mind and eventually agrees to some desirable compromise. We as younger people are usually busy, perhaps with a job, family and home to run, and it is a great temptation to see what needs doing and do it, simply in the interests of saving time. It is undoubtedly more efficient to work this way, but bossily taking over your remaining parent's life can be a great indignity for her, and will do nothing for her morale – or, following on from that, her physical welfare, if she is in full command of her faculties and capable of considering and making decisions.

You may be one of those people who feels quite confident coping with practical matters but finds helping a parent to cope with her bereavement, come to terms with it and rebuild her personality much more difficult. If

43

the person who has died was your own mother or father (rather than an in-law), you will be experiencing many of the same deep emotions of grief and loss yourself. Everyone reacts differently. Jane, for instance, said that she felt 'frozen inside' when her mother died. She was unable to cry or express her shock and grief, though she felt she could say the right words and comfort her father adequately and deal with all the things that had to be done at the time. It is important, for an older person, particularly, to go through a period of mourning in order to be able to accept that the beloved partner has gone, then welcome back all the happy memories that are left and rebuild emotional links with family and friends as a whole personality in his or her own right.

Grief provokes different reactions in different people. Jane's father, for example, felt that his wife had betrayed him by dying and leaving him, and he later went through a period of great resentment against her, which manifested itself in strange ways: he cut down the trees she had planted and loved, for example, and pulled up her forget-me-not bed. But by the time of his own death four years later, he had come to terms with his loss and remembered her happily with all the love and affection they had shared in their life together.

It was Jane's husband, however, who was the greatest help to her widowed father. In-laws can often comfort more adequately – because while they have known the dead person well, they are not as emotionally involved as their husband or wife. A sympathetic, patiently objective approach from an in-law can be very helpful.

If your widowed parent wants to continue independent and live on her own, she will almost certainly find a great change in her social life. If your parents are both still living, anything you can do to encourage the formation of separate outside interests will be a very good investment for the future, so that if one of them is eventually left alone he or she will have at least a nucleus of friends, somewhere to go and something to do that is familiar. Although many married couples, friends of your parents, will 'stick' to the parent who is left, others will not. Some people feel that three is an awkward number or even feel jealousy of the unattached person who has been left behind. A widow or widower is also a constant reminder of bereavement, which they find too painful to contemplate very often, particularly as many bereaved people need the emotional release of going through their partner's last illness and death time and again to anyone who will listen.

Personalities vary considerably, of course, and it will pay to be sensitive to what your surviving parent was like before his or her loss. In the case of a mother, she may have been a helpless woman, whose very fragility and inability to cope were part of her charm for her husband, who may have enjoyed being a dominant partner in the home. This makes it very difficult for you, as carer, as you will not be able to supply the protection and help she had from him, both physically and emotionally. However, you will have to try to give, or organize, as much support as you possibly can during the first period of mourning, and very gently ease her into doing more for herself as time goes on. She may be quite incapable, because of her nature, of taking on much at first. Moreover the rebuilding of her personality and self-confidence may take quite some time.

It is often easier if a strong and active person has been left on her own, but you may find that she tends to do *too* much, and throws herself into exhausting bouts of housecleaning, gardening, re-decorating and so on quite early after losing her husband. This is one way of working through one's grief, and while you will want to ensure that she gets adequate rest and does not do so much that she suffers physical damage, you will probably have to let her get on with it and organize things to her own satisfaction.

It is said that it takes at least a year for a bereaved person to return to anything like normal – and for some older people, the process can be much slower. The period after the loss can see a great variety of reactions, ranging from sleeplessness to minor illnesses, lack of interest in food, loss of weight and depression. When Maureen lost her husband, who was more than twenty years her senior, after nursing him for two years through cancer, her own physical health deteriorated alarmingly. She was completely worn out emotionally and living on tranquillizers and sleeping tablets, without which she could get no rest at all. She had lost all interest in food and was very thin. Having no children of her own, she found one of her greatest supporters was her husband's daughter by a first marriage, and other relatives and friends rallied round. It took her quite two years to get back to normal.

Returning to the subject of food, it is important to ensure that your parent is having an adequate diet of the right foods, particularly as living alone removes the incentive of cooking for two and the pleasure of eating in company. If you are living nearby, it will be easier to keep an eye on things, but if you are at a distance, you will have to call in some help.

If you can find out about lunch clubs, often run by voluntary organizations or as part of the social services network, and persuade your parent to go along one or two days a week (transport is often provided), this will help her to meet new friends, have a hot meal at a reasonable price, and be in the company of others while she is eating. Perhaps there is a congenial elderly neighbour who might like to come to some arrangement such as having a meal with her, perhaps in one house one week and the other the next. Meals-on-wheels can be a lifeline as far as getting adequate food to the old person is concerned, but constant meals without company can be as unappetizing as meals without salt.

Think through the possible problems of obtaining food, if your parent lives some distance away and is ill or if the weather is very bad. Do any of her local shops deliver? Does the milkman carry groceries as well as milk? (This can be a real bonus, as anyone who has been confined to the house with sick small children knows.) Is there a neighbour who could help, either by doing some shopping or offering a lift? If your parent has a home help, will she be able to fit in a little shopping?

Your mother will, of course, have been used to planning meals and shopping for two or more all her married life and you will have a sound basis on which to plan a food budget together. It may be more difficult for your father, who has probably been used to eating whatever was put in front of him and may not have any experience of cooking. James (see pages 26-31) was greatly in favour of convenience foods for his old parents, and there is much to be said for them provided they are chosen properly and form part of a good balanced diet.

Give your father a rough guide as to what nutritionists recommend as this 'good balanced diet' (it may be better to put it over in this impersonal way!).

Half a pint of milk a day, some fruit, protein in the form of a portion of meat, eggs, fish, cheese or chicken, vegetables or salad, wholemeal bread (if you can persuade him to eat it: many elderly men prefer white bread) and cereal with natural fibre will be adequate. Prepare some sample menus, keeping the preparation and cooking as easy as possible, and if possible using such dishes as a casserole or large piece of chicken or small roast for two days' meals. (See suggestions below.)

Suggest basic stores which can be kept for emergency, being 'turned over' and used from time to time and replaced. The following would provide several meals if your parent were unable to go out (the list assumes no refrigerator or freezer – if he has the latter, of course, he could be provided with entire meals ready to heat and eat):

dried, canned or long-life milk;

Oxo or Bovril for drinks or adding to stews and casseroles;

small jar of coffee and packet of tea to be kept for emergencies;

canned fruit juice;

canned or packet soups;

sweet and plain biscuits (stored in a tin);

cans of meat and fish (corned beef, stewed steak, tuna, sardines, etc.);

canned meat pie or steak-and-kidney pudding;

vegetables (dried peas or beans, canned carrots, tomatoes, red kidney beans, baked beans, etc.);

canned fruit;

canned custard and rice pudding or other milk pudding;

instant mashed potato (look out for the kind with added vitamin C);

canned new potatoes.

(Remember that two small cans are more useful than one

large one.) The above provides a basis for preparing meals in emergency or as a time- and trouble-saver. It would be easy, for instance, to use a can of stewed meat with one of carrots added to it, make a portion of instant mash or open a small can of potatoes, and follow it with canned fruit and custard (any custard left over could be used next day with a sliced fresh banana).

If you are not around, try to get a friend or local helper (perhaps a home help) to keep a discreet eye on how your parent is eating, perhaps by checking the rubbish bin or store cupboard from time to time.

One of the problems of cooking for one is that it is uneconomical in its use of fuel and unless your parent has a freezer it is no use making, say, a large casserole or cooking a whole chicken. He may not object to eating it two days running, but will not want to do so for several days on end. There are various ways of saving gas and electricity. A small slow-cooker, which uses very little electricity, can make good one-pot meals. These cookers are surprisingly versatile in what they can cook, too (read the instructions before buying, to check). There are also some good stacking pans now on the market which can cook a whole meal in three separate pans on one gas or electric ring.

If your parent has been used to using a pressure cooker, this will also save money, but it may not be possible to introduce one as a new gadget at this stage; many elderly people are nervous of them if they have not been used to them before.

Remind your parent that cold meals are just as nutritious as hot ones, though to the elderly hot food can often seem more comforting. Perhaps if he is having salad or sandwiches, a hot bowl of soup beforehand will be enjoyed, or a canned steamed pudding to follow, with a heated-up can of custard. Sandwiches can be toasted – even a relatively boring cheese sandwich becomes a bit more special and enjoyable if it has been popped under the grill.

Suggestions for recipe books and booklets are given on page 221, but the gift of such books too soon could in itself be depressing to your parent, underlining as it does the fact that he or she is now alone. It might be better to obtain a book yourself and pass on the ideas and recipes as appropriate. Cookbooks for students (in which recipes are sure to be cheap and easy as well as interesting) or for cooking in a bed-sit (for meals that are cheap on fuel and simple to prepare) are also worth plundering.

Remember to check, if your parent is living alone, that he or she can still cope with a gas cooker. These are available to buy or rent fitted with safety devices to make them less hazardous for elderly or disabled people to use – check with the local gas board. Financial help with the provision of a safer cooker may be available if your parent is on supplementary pension. In certain regions gas boards will carry out regular safety inspections on pensioners' gas appliances.

Overleaf will be found some suggestions for a week's easy-to-prepare menus which might appeal to an elderly person. Many elderly people prefer to have their main meal in the middle of the day and a light tea/supper as they find it easier to sleep if they have not had a heavy meal recently, and these menus reflect this preference. However, they may of course be changed round as desired.

Breakfasts can be fairly standard throughout the week, but it can be boring to get up and know that you are in for the same old packet of cereal day after day. It might be a good idea to buy packs of small one-portion packets of different cereals, together with a small packet of All-Bran to sprinkle on for additional fibre, and a small packet of a good muesli. Half a banana or orange sliced up and added to cereal can make it more appetizing. Also, don't forget that you can use orange juice with cereal instead of milk. In winter, if your parent can take the trouble, porridge with brown sugar, golden syrup or honey makes a change from cereal. In addition, he could have toast with butter or margarine and jam, marmalade or honey. An old-fashioned treat some of our grandparents enjoyed and which would make a pleasant summer breakfast is toast buttered lightly and spread with thinly sliced tomatoes sprinkled with a tiny amount of sugar. Or try another toast-and-fruit combination – hot buttered toast eaten with a peeled and quartered ripe, juicy pear. Plus, of course, tea or coffee as preferred.

SUNDAY
Lunch
Small pack of frozen lean roast beef with gravy; baked potato; vegetables according to season
Fresh fruit salad – small apple wiped, cored and diced, small orange peeled and sliced, few grapes pipped and peeled with half a can of custard
Supper
Poached egg on toast, small bought fruit pie

MONDAY
Lunch
Half grapefruit (eat other half for Tuesday's breakfast)
2 chicken pieces, grilled (save one for next day); portion of instant mash or fresh boiled potatoes; frozen peas
A few sweet biscuits
Supper
Cheese and tomato on toast, popped under grill to brown
1 banana sliced and mixed with remaining half can of custard

TUESDAY
Lunch
Flesh off remaining piece of chicken diced and mixed with mayonnaise and a little curry powder, if liked; lettuce or watercress and tomato salad; canned new potatoes
Pastry or fruit pie
Supper
Sardines on toast
Blancmange or milk jelly

WEDNESDAY
Lunch
Piece of pork sparerib; baked potato; vegetables in season
Piece of fruit
Supper
Cheese and biscuits, with pickle or other garnish
Small can rice pudding and jam

THURSDAY
Lunch
Canned corned beef (keep any left over); salad; boiled potatoes

Canned treacle pudding and custard (save half for next day)
Supper
Scrambled egg on toast, with mushrooms
Piece of fruit

FRIDAY
Lunch
Bought fish and chips, with a portion of peas cooked at home
Fruit yoghurt if liked, or portion of ice cream
Supper
Corned-beef sandwiches with tomato
Rest of treacle pudding and custard

SATURDAY
Lunch
Mince, cooked with onion and thickened, and made into shepherd's pie with instant mash; green vegetable
Instant pudding made with milk
Supper
Toast and meat paste with salad garnish
Bought cream cake or pastry

   Last thing at night, your parent could have a milk drink of some kind and a biscuit if liked. It is unrealistic to think that elderly people will do without such things as sweet biscuits, sweets and chocolates altogether or that they will always eat wholemeal bread if they have not been used to it, or that they will always have fresh fruit where recommended instead of pudding. These suggestions do not include cooking directions, but this is where you or another carer could help. Of course, tea and coffee can be taken as desired, and fresh fruit juice too, but small cartons are a better buy than large ones, as once opened the vitamin C content quickly deteriorates.
   It is a good idea to 'build in' dishes or foods that your parent particularly likes and to put in the occasional treat such as a bought cream cake or portion of fish and chips or some other convenience food which may not be the acme of health-promoting perfection but will stimulate the appetite, give the elderly person something to look forward to and add zest to the week's menu.

Provided your parent is keeping reasonably fit, and you are satisfied that she is receiving plenty of company (even if you can visit only from time to time), there are one or two things you should look out for. Even if she is well and active, the task of, for instance, spring cleaning the house may seem very daunting to her (after all, it is quite exhausting enough when one is young and fit). This may be something a voluntary organization can give her a hand with, or you may be able to rally round with members of the family to go through the house and do some re-decorating. Or it may be more convenient for someone to go on a regular day, say every fortnight, prepared to tackle some cleaning jobs throughout the year. Being able to keep the house as clean and tidy as it used to be is a great morale-booster, and the pleasure of company at the same time is also good.

A home help can be provided in some circumstances, if necessary. First, a supervisor will come round to chat to your parent to see how much help and of what kind she will need and to help her fill in the application forms (see Chapter 12). Payment is in accordance with means. The service is sympathetically run, and the supervisor will try to supply someone who will be congenial and whom the elderly person will like. It can be a great boon to carers to know that there will be a regular helping hand, someone to do the shopping, lift and clean under heavy furniture, and so on; often extremely good relationships are formed between the old person and her 'help' (see Alice's case history, pages 186–7).

Your parent may have had a pet or pets when her partner was alive, and if so, the animal's presence may well prove a great blessing, as well as welcome company, in her widowhood. The fact that some creature depends on her for its food and well-being can be a tremendous help in taking her out of her grief. Some medical authorities say that a dog or cat is positively beneficial to people with heart conditions in that stroking and petting it can relax the invalid and relieve strain on the heart. If your parent likes animals but has no pet, it might be an idea to consider buying her a suitable one for a Christmas or birthday present. Even a budgie, which takes little caring for, can prove an entertaining little pet and good companion. But it is important to discuss this first with your parent – she may really be against the idea and not want to be bothered, in which case it would be a mistake to impose an animal on her. However, in some areas of Britain, volunteers visit old people in their homes or in residential care and take their dogs along, and these visits are apparently much appreciated by people who can no longer keep their own pet.

If your parent already has a pet, discreetly make sure that it is not proving too much of a burden for him or her to cope with alone. A young dog, for instance, may need more exercise than your parent can give it, and it may be necessary to organize help in taking it for walks or even, in an extreme case, finding it a new home, preferably where your parent can visit it.

One of the main problems of an elderly person living alone – however much satisfaction he or she may get from being independent and able to cope single-handedly – is isolation. In spite of the many opportunities that now exist for all kinds of educational and social activities for different age-groups, it can often take a strong incentive to make an elderly parent go out and take advantage of them, and meet people of her own generation with whom she can share memories or a group of mixed-age people with the same interests as herself. Increasing frailty, the fear of falling over or of coming home alone in the dark can all contribute to this reluctance; or, having had the support of a partner for many years, she may feel unsure of her ability to mix with other people as a person in her own right, perhaps not even wanting to enter a room on her own.

If your parent is handicapped in some way she may of course be unable to go out on her own. Many elderly people suffer greatly from loneliness and may be on their own for two or three days at a time without a visitor. Disorientating enough for a young, fit person, this can have an even worse effect on an old person, perhaps causing confusion and lasting mental deterioration. The telephone is certainly a lifeline for many old people, though tact and patience may be needed on the part of the carer to keep the old person's calls within bounds. And of course unhurried visits, with two-way conversations in which you speak *to* your parent and not *at* him or her are better than just 'popping in' to check that all is well and dashing off again. There are sad stories of old people actually enhancing a disability in hospital so that they would not have to be discharged and return to the loneliness of home again. Such behaviour is probably unconscious on the part of the people concerned, but nevertheless expresses a very real fear.

It is necessary, then, to assess from time to time, and from this point of view, how your parent is coping on his or her own. He may have been brought up in a large family where there were always people bustling to and fro and may have enjoyed company on a casual basis all the time. For him isolation could be a very real problem, and circumstances he would consider lonely and quiet might be regarded by someone else brought up as an only child as a reasonably social existence punctuated by a fair number of visits and outings. You will know the background of your particular parent, and your assessment of his new lifestyle on his own will contribute to later decisions as to whether he will come to live with you or whether he might be happier in a residential home where there is always something going on and people to-ing and fro-ing.

Sometimes the causes of isolation are very obviously physical. Deafness, for instance, can effectively cut people off even from their nearest and dearest. Not all old people will admit that their hearing is getting worse and this, of course, makes things doubly difficult if they will not agree to get help in the form of a hearing aid. Blindness or impaired sight is clearly another great cause of isolation. Try to avoid, in such cases, the common tendency to shout and speak with exaggerated simplicity to people with hearing or optical disabilities as if their understanding were also impaired.

Apart from encouraging your parent to go out as much as possible, and seeing that she is visited regularly (apart from visits by social worker, district nurse or home help, which, though valuable, are basically for some other purpose than that of providing company), think of other ways in which your parent can keep occupied and interested at home. As well as television, which does provide a human voice and face, make sure he has a small radio to which he can listen in bed when he wakes in the morning. If he has always enjoyed reading, perhaps you could collect some magazines for him and take them in regularly, and make sure he sees a newspaper every day. These are an expensive item nowadays, particularly for someone on a small income, but a neighbour may be able to drop his paper through the letterbox in the evening for your parent to enjoy. Perhaps there is someone who can change library books for him, if the library is difficult for him to visit, having discussed with him what sort of books he likes.

One piece of equipment your mother or father might enjoy, if not worried by the thought of working new-fangled gadgets, is a tape recorder. These have now come down in price considerably and would make an excellent joint family present. Your parent could tape as much as he or she can remember of the family history, which would make fascinating listening, or have a conversation about it with other family members on the same subject. Or she might like to record favourite music from the radio or record a 'letter' to send to distant friends or relatives. One grandfather we knew, who lived two hundred miles from his little grandchildren, used to tape bedtime stories for them – the same stories which had delighted his own daughter when she was a small girl.

However fit and well your lone parent seems to be, it is prudent to make some contingency plans in case he is suddenly taken ill, falls victim to a stroke, or whatever. To avoid upsetting him and making him think that you have found out from his doctor something about his health that he does not know, it is best to make some simple preparations yourself and if necessary enlist the help of a friendly neighbour. Pack a small bag with spare dressing-gown, slippers, pyjamas, toilet items and shaving tackle, and so on (or the feminine equivalent if it is for your mother), some change for telephone calls and anything else you think could be useful, and put it away in your house or the neighbour's just in case of emergency. It could save a great deal of anxious dashing about should the occasion suddenly arise when he has to go into hospital.

CATHY

Cathy, who is divorced, was living with her children of 15 and 16½ and working part-time when caring for her mother became a problem. Over a period of a couple of years, she noticed a gradual deterioration. Then her mother started to stay in bed a great deal. Cathy found the situation very worrying, not least because her mother lived sixty miles away and visiting was difficult. The problem, never out of Cathy's mind, made her feel very lonely and depressed, although she hoped that as the weather improved, so would her mother's condition. In fact, it did not.

The first thing Cathy did was to obtain a home help for her mother. Also, as she was unable to get to the shops, which were half a mile away, she was able to have meals-on-wheels. Subsequently, for a short period, the district nurse came in for a brief period morning and afternoon.

Cathy was in the process of creating her own business – a rest home for elderly people – and had moved to the south coast in order to do so, although she did not live on the premises of the rest home, but in her own house. Her mother had a bad fall and went into hospital for six weeks, then to another rest home and finally, when it was ready and there was a place for her, to Cathy's own rest home.

Cathy realized she had been fortunate in that she was 'in the business' and that her case was not therefore typical of offspring with dependent parents. As she said, with the founding of the rest home, her business life changed, but her social and family life did not. She was lucky that one of her daughters helped a great deal with the rest home, and she really felt that for her mother to stay there was the best solution for the whole family as well as for the old lady.

'After all,' she told me, 'the age gap was so great. My mother was 90, I was 51 and the children were 15 and 16. I have seen in other families that there can often be resentment if an old person is brought into the home as old people are in the main very selfish – like children. If they require looking after they can contribute very little to the family who have been used to being on their own. It generally does not work.

'From my experience in running the rest home, I learned a lot about caring for the elderly. I'd say if you have to do it, be positive, be relaxed and be natural. Make sure the old person knows the family timetable and that you need time alone.

Encourage her to do as much for herself as is safe and foster independence – do not always include her in your social life.

'If there is loss of memory, learn to "switch off" if she makes an absurd remark. Answer normally, but change the subject. And if wandering is the problem, it's essential to put address labels in the pockets and/or the handbag. Incontinence is difficult to cope with, but with medical aids this is manageable if hard work. Try to treat the patient as normal so that you don't heighten the nervousness which can make the situation worse. Don't think you are looking after a parent, but rather that you have added another child to the family.*

'I do feel that more could be done in educating people to treat the elderly firmly but without depriving them of their dignity. They do not, in my experience, like to make decisions, although of course every case is different. We probably had residents in the home who were less capable than many of taking any initiative. It's very important to make sure that your parent continues to wash properly, has her hair done, visits the chiropodist, and so on – and, above all, has a regular routine and the pleasure of as frequent "treats" as you can manage.*

'In the case of my own mother, I did not use any voluntary organizations, but perhaps my situation was rather a special one, as I had gone professionally into the caring business. The official "helpers" such as the DHSS, hospitals and social services I found magnificent and unfailingly courteous.'*

LENA

Lena's mother died over twenty years ago, having suffered a stroke and been ill for a number of years. Lena always regretted that she was not able to look after her, but she herself suffered a serious illness at about the same time so was unable to do very much to help.

After her mother's death, she saw very little of her father, an academic, with whom she had never got on very well. She found him very aggressive and domineering when she was a child and only realized when she had married and had her own four children that, in fact, he had never really wanted children but wished to be the sole object of his wife's attention himself.

Suddenly, two years ago, Lena received a phone call out of the blue from the woman in whose house her father was living (he was 86 by then), to say that he was in hospital and that there was no way she could continue to look after him when he came out (she was 85 herself and, in fact, suffered a stroke a short time later).

'There was nothing I could do but take responsibility,' said Lena. 'I packed up and took off for his home 60 miles away from mine. I realized that I couldn't give him the full-time care that he would need myself, and that I'd have to apply all my energies to finding the very best possible home where he could stay.

'It was a truly appalling experience. Some places were so obviously just out to make money and really didn't care for the people who were living there. In one place, which was actually recommended by the social services, my daughter (who came to help me) and I found an old lady sitting by herself shouting in a darkened room – and no one came to her aid. We nearly tripped over a piece of torn carpet on the landing there. Another home, run by a voluntary organization, was highly regulated, with outings and visits and lots of activity, but the people in it were sitting lined up round the room, had to eat in the entrance hall and had no privacy when eating or sleeping. And frankly, the place smelt. Another place we visited was very good and had everything we were looking for – but it also had a waiting list of two years! However, it did take my father in for a couple of weeks while we continued our search.

'At last we found somewhere suitable, just when we were ready to give up. The local paper carried a survey of homes, and a new one just starting up was advertised there. The social services denied all knowledge of it, and I don't know to this day if it has been registered and inspected. However, we saw it and were impressed – the woman running it was the sort of person you can trust and like, and it only has six guests. Each person has their own room and there are plenty of staff to care for them – and they really do seem to care. There are separate small dining tables, not an institutional long table, there's a bar, and wine is served with dinner on Saturday nights.

'My father loves the place. He's quite a loner, which is fortunate as the company is perhaps not quite intellectual enough for him! But he wanders into the kitchen to get himself a glass of milk at night, and the staff all treat him with affection and liking. I am able to go and see him once a month, and on the occasions I have stayed there I've been very

*impressed with the food and standard of caring. We have to
pay, of course, and if we did not receive help we couldn't
afford it, but frankly I don't see how the management of the
home can give the standard of care they do for the fees they
charge.*

*'However, the greatest bonus for me has been the fact that
since my father was taken ill he and I have started to get on so
well. It was really when he stopped having to be my father,
and our relationship in a sense became reversed. He no longer
bosses me about. When I took him on holiday to Switzerland
last year, he woke up one morning and didn't know where he
was. Eventually he wandered into my room and said, "I
thought I would find my mother here" – very revealing, don't
you think?*

*'I was really handed my father on a plate, and I took out a
power of attorney so that I could deal with his affairs. I would
recommend anyone in the same position to consult a good
solicitor and get the legal and financial side sorted out. He is
just now beginning to fail, and has had a serious illness
(cancer), so I think it would be as well for me to take out an
Enduring Power of Attorney under the new Act, so that if his
mental faculties are impaired I can still manage things for him.*

*'From my experience, I would advise anyone looking for a
home for their parent to be really nosey: don't just put your
head round the door and don't simply look at the rooms and
facilities that the people running the home want you to look
at. Pry a bit – go with a friend or relative so that while one of
you makes conversation the other can wander off and look at
the kitchen, bedrooms, etc. After all, you will be paying a good
deal of money for the home, especially if, like my father's, it is
private, and you are entitled to feel you and your parent are
getting good value. As I said before, I really don't know if the
home my father is in is recognized – I feel I would rather trust
my own judgement over whether a place is good or not.'*

CHAPTER 4

Homes from home?

It is probably one of the hardest decisions you will have to face – whether to have your mother or father (or both) to live with you, or go and live with them, or whether to try to find sheltered accommodation or a home for them.

Many factors will influence you: how infirm your parent is and how much in need of specialized nursing; how much space there is in your own home or theirs; the attitude of the rest of the family; the elderly person's attitude and feelings; money and other resources available; and perhaps most important of all, your own attitude and assessment of yourself, if you would be the main carer.

Could you cope, both mentally and physically, with a very demanding job from which it would be difficult to opt out and of an unknown duration? Would you have to give up a career which you prize not only for the money it brings in (and this is a great consideration) but also for its satisfaction? Could you regard the elderly relative as an asset to the family, rather than a liability? Looking at the situation as a whole, would it seem more important for a younger couple with perhaps 20 more years of career and active life in front of them to be able to sustain their relative freedom of operation or for the elderly person to live with his own family in his declining years? Would moving him into some kind of home or sheltered flat instead be seriously detrimental to his quality of life? After all, looked at dispassionately and on a scale of points, there is little doubt whose life, or lives, would suffer the greatest disruption by a decision to take the old person into the family home and keep the caring in the family.

The variables are, of course, enormous and the relationships involved can be infinitely complicated. It is certainly not a decision which should be taken for granted by anyone concerned, but should be thoroughly discussed by all interested parties, and, if necessary, with your own and/or your parent's GP, someone from the social services or some other impartial but responsible person outside the family. Many people I talked to said, 'I couldn't have lived with myself if I'd not taken her in' – or a variation on this theme. But others quite freely admitted that if they had realized the problems involved they would at least have thought longer and harder about it and perhaps made some other provisions, even if their final decision had been the same.

The newspaper 'agony aunt' Marjorie Proops answered a letter from a desperate reader of 51, who had been undergoing the 'change' with all its attendant symptoms, was worried that her husband was seeing another woman, and was trying to cope with her mother, who lived with her and her husband and was ill and incontinent. At the end of her tether, the reader put her mother into a home, but her mother hated it and blamed her daughter – who also blamed herself. Suddenly the mother died and the daughter felt desperately guilty that she might have hastened her end. This woman, as Marjorie Proops rightly commented, could not in the circumstances have made a good job of caring for her mother or given her the nursing she needed, and certainly she was not in any way responsible for her mother's death. She also observed how many middle-aged daughters are faced with and will be faced with a similar dilemma. The situation was similar to many I encountered while researching this book, and many people who *have* taken it upon themselves to look after parents in their own homes have said: 'I'd never blame anyone for putting a parent into a home. Some people are in circumstances or have problems which make them quite unable to cope. I was lucky and could cope.'

Let us suppose you have decided to take your parent in, or maybe to move into your parent's home. If your relationship is basically good and affectionate, give or take the odd arguments which can inevitably crop up among close relatives, and, assuming you are married and have your own family, your husband and children are willing to be supportive and helpful, the outlook is not all gloom and doom. One of the most important factors is having enough space, or being able to create it by building an extension, converting a garage to living quarters, or whatever. Access to privacy – for both the older person and yourself – is essential.

Good local support can also make a great difference, whether from the social services, voluntary bodies or both. Is transport available, either in your family or from volunteers, to take your parent to medical appointments, luncheon clubs, to visit friends, and so on? How willing and able are you when it comes to nursing a sick parent, dealing with incontinence, or a habit of wandering off, and so on? And how good is your own health? Would extra physical and mental strain have an adverse effect on you? Good health and an equable temperament are priceless assets in such situations. What about money? Would you have to give up your own job, and have you worked out allowances, etc. to check just how you would manage? Adequate finance is not everything, but it can certainly provide a firm foundation for a successful caring venture.

When you are in the process of weighing up the pros and cons, you should investigate what is available locally in the way of alternative care. Just as if you were planning to return to work after having a baby and were looking for a babysitter or child-minder to look after your child, you would explore all the possibilities and try to find the best possible care, so you should check on what is available for older people. Even if you do not need the facilities immediately, there may come a time when you do, and you will be glad you have found out as much as possible. Let us consider some of the alternatives.

Sheltered housing This usually consists of a group of flats or bungalows, each self-contained, in a modern development, where elderly people can take their own furniture, do their own catering and generally be independent (often, too, they may take a pet, but this point should always be checked in advance). Generally there is a common room and communal laundry, and sometimes accommodation is available for visiting relatives too.

The main advantage of sheltered housing, however, is that there is a warden who oversees the residents – not interfering, but keeping an eye on everything. She will make sure that the accommodation is well maintained, see that communal rooms and other areas are cleaned and perform small services such as helping out with form-filling, collecting prescriptions and perhaps arranging communal entertainments such as card games. The warden should also know something about her charges' medical history, who their doctors are, and so on, and will usually be able to arrange temporary nursing care if necessary. In case of emergency, she will know how to cope and be able to alert relatives. The feeling of reassurance that a good warden can give is one of the most valuable assets of sheltered housing.

There are several types of sheltered housing. The local authority or a housing association will be able to provide information for your area. The local authorities usually need a residence qualification before they can consider someone for their schemes, although the practical advantages of bringing someone to live in the same area as his or her offspring could exert some influence in the case of a parent who is not resident in the area concerned. To register, the applicant should first fill in the relevant form or forms (the local housing officer will help with this if there are difficulties). If there are specially urgent problems, it is a good idea to attach a brief note saying what these are, plus a letter from the applicant's doctor specifying medical condition and individual needs. Then a housing officer will visit to assess the applicant's present housing accommodation. If your parent is put on the waiting list, he or she will receive a registration card and will be contacted if and when accommodation becomes available.

Housing associations can also provide 'sheltered' homes to rent; tenants are usually chosen according to need and whether they satisfy the association's requirements. The first step is to write to find out who is eligible to apply and whether there is a waiting list or vacancies. Write to Age Concern (see Chapter 12) or ask at your local Age Concern office to find out which associations have accommodation in the relevant area. Housing advice centres or local authority housing departments should also have information on schemes in the areas they cover, but if there is urgent need contact a social worker and take it from there. As to rent, housing associations' charges are determined by a local rent officer, who assesses a fair rent. Rents are reviewed every two years. If their financial circumstances warrant it, tenants of sheltered schemes are eligible to claim housing benefit towards their rent and rates. If a tenant fails to do what his or her tenancy requires, he or she must be given four weeks' notice in writing and may not be evicted without a court order.

Some large building contractors are now building groups of houses or flats suitable for old people, so it is worth enquiring locally if any are planned for the area you have in mind. At the time of writing, for example, Barratts have eleven retirement developments of one- and two-bedroom apartments costing from about £26,000 upwards.

Residential hotels and foster homes If the elderly person is not too infirm and the area is right, may be possible for him or her to live permanently in a hotel, occupying a private room and eating in the communal dining-room. The snag is that some hotels expect their winter residents either to move out during the summer, when higher prices can be charged, or pay the higher charges in order to remain. For this reason you should insist on your parent obtaining an agreement in writing from the hotel manager to state that he or she can stay there permanently. This is by no means true 'sheltered housing', in that the hotel staff are under no obligation to keep an eye on their elderly permanent residents, so it will be necessary to make sure that you or someone else checks periodically that your relative is well or, if not, is receiving the proper attention from doctor, health visitor or district nurse. The organization GRACE (see Chapter 12) will supply a list of residential homes and nursing homes, together with some hotels and guest houses in over twenty counties in southern England. However, the latter are only a small part of the company's business, because there are so few which provide suitable care for elderly residents. All the places on its list have been visited by GRACE's staff and further information is supplied on an individual basis according to the requirements of the enquirer. The organization's registration fee, currently £15, is refundable when a client is accommodated in a residence suggested by GRACE.

Another alternative is foster care, but this is not very widespread. The elderly person who is fostered becomes, in effect, part of a family and is taken in on a paying-guest basis. Some schemes are run by voluntary organizations, while others are under the wing of the local social services department. Payment is usually negotiable with the family offering the accommodation. If the idea appeals to you and your relative, check with a local Age Concern office to see whether such a scheme exists in the required area.

Old people's homes These homes may be known as residential homes, communal homes or rest homes. They exist to provide accommodation for elderly people who can lead a fairly independent life and do not have to have a qualified nurse in charge or on the staff. They are not equipped for nursing people who are immobile, incontinent, confused or who have other disabilities, but most will take in people who, at the most, require a little help with dressing or need a simple diet.

If there is any choice, try to ensure that the home is not too far from shops, post office, public transport, entertainment and so on, and that the other residents would be congenial. Residents should be able to take in at least some of their personal treasures. A home which caters for both sexes will usually have a better atmosphere and will seem less institutional than a single-sex one. If both parents are to go into the home, it is essential to make sure that provision exists for married couples. Also, check whether senile and medical cases are mixed within the home: in the better ones they are not, because the attendance required, and the general atmosphere generated by each type of patient, is very different.

Take your parent with you to look at the home in question and try to reassure him or her about it. The advantages (of good homes) to bring to your relative's attention are that residents are able to retain their independence and may be visited by their relatives and friends as if in their own home. If they fall ill, they will be looked after, and usually their time is their own. Mealtimes will be set, but otherwise the day will not be regimented. Often entertainments and occupations are organized but there is no obligation for residents to join in. If the home is in the same area as the one where your relative lived before, he or she will be able to retain the same doctor.

Some homes are run by local authorities, some by voluntary bodies, others are private. Local authority homes are usually for old people living in the area and applications should be made through the social services department. On receipt of an application a social worker will visit to assess the old person's need for a place and will bring an application form. This will be quite comprehensive, covering, for example, family circumstances, physical condition of the applicant, financial resources (pensions, annuities, social security benefits, etc.) and whether the applicant owns his or her own home. As there is usually a considerable waiting list for places, the social worker may arrange for extra assistance in the meantime, such as meals on wheels or a home help; if further problems arise, the social worker may be contacted immediately in case there is a chance that the admission can be brought forward. Once the place has been offered and accepted, it is important to make your parent feel that the move will be to his or her advantage. Local authorities are now much better at public relations and will do their best to make residents feel at home, as far as possible; some even produce a letter of welcome containing information about the homes and how they are run.

All authorities fix a standard charge for their residential accommodation, which varies according to region. The amount residents actually pay varies, too, according to individual financial circumstances, as assessed by the social worker and recorded on the applicant's form. The payment covers board and lodging and essential services such as laundry. In addition, there are various financial schemes which may be entered into, and allowances which may be claimed. The social worker will explain how these work.

Private homes choose their own residents from applicants and of course their charges are comparatively high. These homes vary in how much nursing care they can offer: some, for example, will not accept cases of mental illness or immobility.

Before making any commitment, check carefully on what is offered for the money, and also whether any grant towards the cost would be forthcoming from the social services department: it would be a pity to have to move your parent from somewhere she is used to and where she is happy simply because her savings have been used up. Sometimes charitable organizations can make grants towards the cost of accommodation in residential homes: again, check with Age Concern or consult the *Charities Digest*.

When considering private homes, it is a good idea to talk to people who have had experience of them and also to check with the local authority, which keeps a list of registered private homes. The authority is obliged to inspect these to make sure that the standards do not fall below specified levels.

Again, GRACE can help with information on what is available (see above). Another organization which provides a national computerized register of accommodation for the elderly, covering sheltered housing, sheltered accommodation, residential care homes, hotels and nursing homes that provide care for the active retired and elderly is Elderly Accommodation Counsel (see address in Chapter 12). There is a charge for the information and applicants are advised to check on the accommodation for themselves once addresses have been supplied by the EAC.

Voluntary organization homes, as the name implies, are those which are run by such organizations as the Salvation Army and other religious bodies. Most of the homes are small, with fewer than forty or fifty residents. The charges vary from home to home and details of applicants' financial circumstances are requested. If an applicant cannot pay the fees, the organization may be able to provide funds to help; alternatively, the local authority may be able to provide a subsidy.

Consult the annual *Charities Digest* for information, or write to the Salvation Army (see Chapter 12) for information about its Eventide Homes (for people of all denominations); alternatively, contact Church of England,

Catholic, Methodist or Jewish central offices, as appropriate, for details of homes for members of each particular faith. These homes, like private ones, are periodically inspected by the local authority to make sure they comply with the current statutory requirements.

STAYING AT HOME

If your parent is not severely incapacitated, it may of course be possible for him or her to continue living at home, with some adaptations and extra help from various sources. Many elderly people are most reluctant to leave the home they have lived in for many years, and indeed, there is a lot to be said for staying in a neighbourhood where you have good friends, a familiar doctor and shops where people greet you by name. However, in some cases the old person's house may be too large, old and difficult to heat and maintain, and a move to a smaller house or flat could offer many advantages: running costs would be lower, and the opportunity to choose a new area, perhaps near relatives or old friends, could prove useful. It might even be possible to opt for a warmer, southern climate, or to exchange a house with stairs for a bungalow.

If the house is a large one, it might be possible for the old person to stay put if, for example, it could be converted into flats. Some housing associations will agree to buy an elderly person's house, convert it into flats and give one to the original owner of the house – a scheme with distinct advantages. Of course, the old person would have to move out while the conversion was taking place, but could perhaps stay with friends or relatives and have the furniture stored during that time.

Help the Aged has a 'Gifted Housing Plan' in which the elderly person donates his or her property to Help the Aged in return for the charity's caring for him/her. The old person would then be housed either in one of the organization's sheltered housing schemes or one of its 'managed residences'. There are four options: to continue living in his/her present home, but be relieved of the worry and expense of external maintenance, insurance and rates; to have the present home converted, if large enough, into flats, one of which could be chosen by the elderly person for his/her own use; to move into a warden-administered flat or bungalow in one of Help the Aged's sheltered housing schemes; or to move into a managed residence, which has no warden but enjoys the management and help of the organization's regional staff. For further details of the scheme, contact Help the Aged (address in Chapter 12).

Alternatively, it might be possible for part of the house to be let, if congenial tenants could be found. There are pitfalls, of course, and a solicitor should first be consulted about the legal aspects, not least the possibilities of removing an unsuitable tenant, tax and other financial obligations which might arise from receiving rent, and so on. Also the elderly person's ability to adapt should be considered: some people get on well with strangers, others do not.

Grants are available for adapting houses, though the regulations and restrictions relating to these can be complicated. Age Concern can advise; alternatively, contact the local council direct to see what improvements and repairs to the house would qualify. No work, however, should be started simply in the hope that a grant will be available.

Otherwise, if finance is available, it might be worth looking at the house objectively with a view to renovating and improving it to accommodate your parent's state of health, disability (if any), and so on. Any improvements could be regarded as a long-term investment for when the property is eventually sold, but the enjoyment of them would be your parent's, who would be able to remain in his or her familiar 'territory'.

Another possibility, which would allow your parent to stay in his or her own neighbourhood but in more suitable accommodation, would be to contact the local housing authority and ask whether it would be interested in buying the house and rehousing your parent elsewhere. This would, of course, depend on how much money the authority had available and what its housing policies were.

Finally, after considering all the other possibilities, you may decide that the best solution is for your parent to come and live with you. The next chapter suggests ways of making the venture a success and the happiest possible time for all concerned.

DELIA

Delia had worked for some years for the social services and therefore had considerable experience of dealing with carers before she became one herself. In some ways she had found her job very disillusioning: it seemed to her that very often people who genuinely needed help were diffident and therefore did not receive it, while others who displayed, as she put it, 'more cunning', did.

Her own mother had been an excellent parent who did everything for her family. When her children grew up, she devoted all her care and attention to her husband. When he died, she was in her seventies, still full of energy and basically a managing woman. She had a few friends, but did not mix much with her neighbours – she came from a background where you tried as far as possible to ignore the fact that there were houses next door, behind the high privet hedges.

Delia realized that the situation might be difficult if her mother came to live with her, her husband and children, so she suggested that her mother go into a sheltered flat – there were some good ones in the neighbourhood. But her mother refused and asked if she could move in with Delia.

'There was no way I could really refuse,' said Delia. 'We had quite a large house, and my mother was able to have her own room and her own furniture, so it should have been ideal for her to be fairly independent and entertain her own friends there.

'However, what I feared would happen did. She was such a bundle of energy that she tried to take over the house! All the books tell you to encourage your parent to spend time in her own room and ask her to do so when your own friends come round, so that you can have some privacy with them. But they don't tell you what to do if your parent refuses, insists on being there all the time when you're entertaining and plies your friends and (in our case) husband's business guests with tales of woe and stories of how badly done by she is!

'Before she came to us, her house was bought by the council and divided into two flats. For a short time my mother lived in

*the ground-floor one, but she didn't like it. There wasn't
enough going on. I remember one day her home help waylaid
me to complain that I never visited my mother and tell me off
about the way I treated her! At the time I was visiting her
three times a week, but the story she had heard from my
mother had sounded so convincing.*

'*After my mother moved in with us, she was always around.
I always found her looking over my shoulder, and I felt so
guilty for resenting it. We couldn't do anything without her
being aware of it. When my daughter got married, Mother
invited everyone she knew to come and see the wedding dress.
We had to laugh about it – that dress was second-hand even
before it had been worn.*

'*Nothing any of us could do was right, and it was particularly difficult for our children, who were teenagers. They
naturally wanted to have their friends in, but Mother would
chase the visitors off if she could. She suffered from diverticulitis, and of course had to have a different diet from the rest of
us, but she accused me of depriving her of the nice food that
we were having! I do think that some people as they get older
become more spiteful, probably because they don't have
sufficient outlet for their energies. This was certainly so in my
mother's case – she wouldn't knit, read or sew – but she
needed mental stimulation which she was incapable of getting
on her own. And she wouldn't listen to our suggestions.*

'*I feel quite strongly that elderly people shouldn't live with
their children's families if it can possibly be avoided. I still feel
guilty about the way I felt about her and wonder if I could
have had more patience, but I did get tired of people saying
how much I had aged after Mother came to live with us. I
don't think people think ahead sufficiently – if you are pretty
sure your parent is going to live with you, you should start
schooling yourself to it as soon as possible, particularly if you
can foresee problems of personality.*

'*We didn't have physical problems, as my mother kept all
her faculties to the end (she was 94 when she died, of a stroke).
But suddenly the unexpected happened. Two ladies called one
day and said they had come to take my mother to show her
over a local old people's home. She had arranged it for herself.
I didn't know what to do. I felt guilty, partly because the relief
was so great but also because the implication was that my care
was inadequate and my mother wasn't happy in my home. But*

71

all my friends said that the decision was hers and that I should let her do what she wanted.

'At first there was a "honeymoon period" and she enjoyed the home, but she soon started to complain. However, she stayed there. I think in some of these homes the old people use their sticks like swords! Of course the homes vary enormously. There are some very well run state ones; some of the [owners of the] private ones I would say are just in it for the money and don't give value. Everyone I've talked to praises the Abbeyfield homes, where you pay according to means. In my view we should copy the idea they have in New Zealand for old people's villages. These have separate bungalows, their own taxis, clubhouse, shops, health centre, etc. Of course, people living there can visit outside and have visitors there, but everything is made very convenient for them [in their home environment]. I do feel something will have to be done about our ageing population in Britain.

'I hope I haven't given too bad an impression of my mother. She was such a good mother and a kind person when she was younger. We did have a lot of laughs about some of the things she got up to. If we hadn't, we'd have gone round the bend! I remember once my husband was painting the window frames and had the window open and a pot of paint standing on the sill. He said to us all, "Mind you don't shut the window, please", and my mother just walked over and, before any of us could do anything, shut it and knocked the paint over so that it spilled inside the room. It seems funny now – but it's a different matter if you're living with that sort of behaviour 24 hours a day.'

CHAPTER 5

Moving in

In your own mind, the decision has been taken. Your mother or father will be coming to live with you and your family, or with you as a single person. You will probably feel relieved that the matter has been decided, and that you will be able to get on with all the practical matters which have to be settled to make the transition as smooth as possible.

MOVING IN WITH THE FAMILY

If there is time, it might be worth having a radical re-think over housing. It is possible that your parent is selling his/her own house or flat before moving in with you. Would she (supposing it is your mother) consider, if your house is suitable, putting the money towards building on an extension or granny annexe (some people now refer to them as grannexes!)? Obviously having designs drawn up, obtaining planning permission and so on would take time, and might have to be done after your parent has moved in with you, but it could be a good arrangement and would allow her to feel that she really had a place of her own, bought with her own money.

Of course, you would all have to be sure that the arrangement was going to work before becoming too heavily committed, and that your parent was quite happy to spend her capital in building the extension, but for many families this has proved a good idea. The parent would probably have left her own house, or money realized from its sale, to her son or daughter on her death anyway, and this would just be a different way of doing so.

The advantage of 'building on', apart from increasing the value of the house, is that the annexe could be designed for the maximum convenience of your parent, to take into account any disabilities she might already have or which might arise in the future. For instance, she could live entirely on ground-floor level, thus eliminating the problem of stairs; convenient heating could be put in, a bathroom could be built with hand rails, an easy-to-enter-and-leave bath, and so on. The annexe could provide privacy for your parent – somewhere she could entertain her friends separately – and privacy for you too, while an alarm bell could be easily installed in case of falls or problems at night.

Some people solve the problem of too little space to take in their parent by putting a mobile home in the garden. You would need consent from local authorities and also from the neighbours to do this, so do investigate before going ahead. Living in a caravan might sound a little primitive, but today's mobile homes can be spacious, well-equipped and very snug. Mains services can be plumbed in and the standard of equipment is very high. A recent holiday in a mobile home in France made me entirely revise my ideas about them. The one we had contained a spacious sitting-/dining-room with gas fire and plenty of built-in shelving and cupboard space, comfortable seating and built-in dining table and benches. The kitchen area was equipped with a stainless-steel sink with water heater, full-size refrigerator and cooker, and cupboards. There was a bathroom with shower, a mains loo and washbasin, and two bedrooms, one of them double. Living with such amenities certainly could not be classed as 'roughing it' – and of course an alarm system and telephone could be installed for an elderly person in case of need and for keeping in touch.

Alternatively, it could be worth your moving to a larger house, putting together the price of your parent's house with what you obtained from the sale of your own. This again could be advantageous to everyone as you would be able to buy a better property with more garden and perhaps more amenities, such as shops nearby, libraries, schools and other facilities. You could look at houses bearing in mind the division of space to accommodate your parent, rather than having to adapt what you have already got, which could be a great advantage.

However, not everyone has a home to sell, and very often accommodation is tight. It can be far from rosy if you have to move two children in together in order to give Gran a room, and such a situation will need very tactful handling. Most of us, fortunately, will not have to face the problems set out in the American television detective series *Cagney and Lacey*. A husband and wife lived with their 12-year-old son in a small two-bedroomed flat. When the wife's mother became immobile through arthritis and came to live with them, the son had to give up his room and sleep on a put-you-up in the living-room, and he was always getting into hot water from his father for playing pop tapes too loudly and leaving his things around. The parents, both of whom went out to work as money was short, were irritable and nervous from constantly having to attend on the old lady, and she herself was unhappy about the whole situation and also in great pain from her disability.

At one point the husband left home, but came back in order to support his wife, though he could not help saying that he thought the old lady would be 'better off dead' for her own sake as her pain was so bad. It is not difficult to foresee the scriptwriter's conclusion: the elderly parent was found smothered in bed in circumstances which implied that a burglar had broken in and stolen her money, but the detectives soon realized from various pointers that the murderer was the small boy. His father's remarks had just tipped the balance and made him feel that he would be doing his grandmother a kindness as well as restoring his parent's marriage and giving him back his room.

It is well worth making every effort at the outset to reconcile everyone concerned to what is being done. Discussion and combined decision-making will serve you better than deciding in your own mind and announcing how the new regime is going to be.

If you have to put two children together in one bedroom, try to divide their shared room so that each has his own area and a certain amount of privacy, even if the division is marked only by a curtain. Giving extra privileges or a special treat or concession may help them over the change – after all, it is a big sacrifice for children to make, however much they love Granny or Grandpa, when they have been used to their own room.

Your partner, too, may find it hard to adjust, even though the parent living with you may be his own. As Alan remarked, 'I'd brought up seven children, and even had grandchildren of my own, but when Mother came to live with us, she still called me "boy" and expected to tell me to wash my hands before dinner and go to church. Mind you, it was just as hard for her, I suppose – I must have seemed a disobedient and difficult child still! Funnily enough, my wife Frances seemed to get on better with her than I did.' The feeling of having to win parental approval can still lurk at the back of the consciousness, and suddenly everyday actions, ways of bringing up the children and social habits and contacts which we know they would not approve of seem to be under the spotlight. A lot of give and take will be needed on both sides (though very often it may seem that the concessions are all on your part), to make the new relationship work, particularly if space is short and it is difficult for the carers to get away.

Sometimes, because of disability or infirmity and because there is nowhere else, the parent's bed has to be set up in the family living-room. This certainly causes severe strain on the rest of the family as normal family activities, the watching of television and the entertaining of friends may all have to be curtailed. Sally's much-loved and highly intelligent grandmother was in this situation, and felt it keenly for her daughter, son-in-law and granddaughter, but there seemed to be no alternative. When her own friends came to visit, she felt she was pushing out her daughter and putting too much work on her as she provided meals, tea and other refreshments.

'As a child, I loved the bustle,' says Sally. 'I liked to see all Gran's friends, uncles and aunts and cousins coming in. I used to sit on her bed and she would read to me, or I'd chat to everyone. It seemed to me to be the centre of the house. In spite of all her pain, Gran was so alive and interested – no one caught her crying in agony but me when everyone else had gone. My parents were too busy trying to catch up with their work. But I realize now what a strain it must have been for them, much as they loved her.'

On the other side of the picture, being ill and incapacitated in full view of everyone is not desirable, so if this is the situation, try to ensure at least some privacy by providing a curtain or screen to hide the bed or make some other arrangement if you possibly can.

PRACTICAL MATTERS

If your elderly parent is moving in, you have a room for her, and everyone is psychologically geared up to give her a good welcome, you should still have a careful look round the house to see whether there are practical ways in which you can make it more convenient for her. Commonsense will probably show you what can be done, but if you need expert help contact the local social services department or a Citizens' Advice Bureau for advice. Here are a few pointers.

If you can give your parent her own room, she will greatly appreciate being able to bring some of her own furniture, especially her bed which she is used to and in which she feels comfortable. She'll need a couple of comfortable chairs, wardrobe and chest of drawers or dressing-table, a radio and portable television and any small bits and pieces which mean 'home' to her. If she can also have an electric kettle and ring so that she can make tea and coffee and cook something in a pan for herself, she will be able to preserve a certain amount of independence. Two cooks in the kitchen all the time could cause problems, but as she has probably been used to cooking all her life and enjoys it, to deprive her of the pleasure entirely would not be a good idea. If you are working all day, and she is hale and hearty enough to prepare an evening meal for everyone, you may, of course, be more than delighted to turn this over to her, and everyone will be pleased. Or let her prepare certain meals in the week for the whole family, cooking her own special dishes.

Look round your home with an eye to safety. Are there any slippery rugs on polished floors? Are the bannisters on the staircase secure? You use slip-resistant polish, of course? Are there any dark corners which could be potentially dangerous, and are your stairs, especially, adequately lit? (Remember to replace that 40-watt bulb with a 100-watt bulb, for example.) Has any of your carpets a curling, lifting edge, or worn bits to trip over?

Heating appliances should be properly serviced and oil heaters placed in a position where they cannot be upset (of course, they must be modern ones with a safety cut-out built in). Electric power points must not be overloaded and electric fires should be well sited to make sure there are no trailing flexes in the middle of the floor. Make sure that there is a fire blanket or a small fire extinguisher available.

If it is some distance to the bathroom from your parent's room consider giving her a commode, if she will accept it, for night use. In any case, look at the bathroom and make sure that it is easy to get in and out of the bath (if not, install a hand rail or stool) and to use the lavatory. Leaving a light on at night is also a good idea.

Make sure that heating is adequate. Hypothermia is a serious problem in the old (see Chapter 9). An electric blanket can be a comfort and there are special low-voltage ones which are good for the elderly. Make sure your parent is not using a hot water bottle at the same time, of course. If there is any doubt about temperature, put a room thermometer in the bedroom to check. If it is less than 60°F/16°C, take action to make sure it is kept warmer. If your parent does not already use one, now might be the time to suggest buying a good duvet. If you have one, she could try it for a night or two – she might then be convinced of its warmth and comfort, and will also appreciate how much easier it is to make the bed in the morning.

Check the garden, too. Is the path uneven or slippery? Is there an outside light? Is there a rail to hold on to if there are outside steps?

Check the ventilation in your parent's room, particularly if there is a gas or solid fuel appliance there. A fireguard would be a good idea if there is an open fire. Make sure that there are no blocked burners or flues and that there is no leaking gas or loose tap.

Your house will be strange at first to the new resident. We all know the feeling of waking up in an unfamiliar place at night and not being able to remember where we are. Ensure that there is a reading lamp with an easily managed switch near the bed, or a torch, if you do not leave a light on on the landing at night.

FAMILY RELATIONSHIPS

When your father or mother moves in with you, try to have a small celebration meal or a drink as a welcome. Remember that, much as your parent may appreciate the security of living with you, and your company, particularly if he/she has been bereaved and is feeling lonely, life with your family will mean a great deal of adjustment, just as his/her presence will to you. Being older, your parent may lack the emotional resources which you have, in your own home and with your own family around you.

Not all old people are easy to get on with, and many have irritating mannerisms and habits or a propensity to criticize. By making concessions at first and showing that you understand what your parent is feeling, you can help him or her to adjust and settle down more easily.

One problem which might arise, quite unexpectedly, is the grandmother who is too uncritical and too full of praise. Recently a young reader wrote to a women's magazine: 'My grandmother lives with us and you couldn't ask for a more lovely person. She was great fun when I was a child, taking me on holidays with her. We used to go to funfairs together and read comics. But she's over eighty now and she can't stop raving about me. She keeps on saying I'm brilliant and tells her friends in front of me how fantastic I am until I feel I could drop through the floor. I dread going into her room because it annoys me so much and I know sometimes I behave coldly towards her, which makes me feel so guilty.' The advice was to joke about it and say, 'Oh yes, of course I'm going to be prime minister one day,' so that the granddaughter's feelings of irritation and anger were de-fused and to remember that it is probably better to have someone living in the house who is full of praise rather than someone who is critical all the time.

On the whole, children and young people have a very good relationship with their grandparents and each generation gets a great deal from the companionship of the other. If you are elderly, being in the company of children can bring back your youth, and your enjoyment with them of books, outings and special occasions such as Christmas will assure you that something of yourself, both inherited and taught, will go on into the future. The children, too, will appreciate the company of someone who has time to spend with them, and they may find they can confide their troubles and problems to a grandparent in the knowledge that they will have a sympathetic audience.

Sally's grandmother, mentioned earlier in this chapter, was, in spite of her profound disability, one of Sally's 'gang'. When Sally was about ten, she used to take her grandmother out in her wheelchair with some of her young friends and they had great fun running the chair down hills and catching it at the bottom, with Granny shouting and laughing with the rest of them. Often the wheelchair had a load of children on it as well as the old lady, all thoroughly enjoying the ride.

Parents may well worry sometimes that the children are being 'spoilt' by their grandparents, but it is necessary to distinguish carefully between love and attention and the undermining of basic and important family rules. There are times when it is wise to turn a blind eye and let the two generations enjoy each other's company, even if a few sweets change hands or you think your child is confiding in someone else and not you. (Yes, a certain amount of jealousy can creep in, too.)

Try to make clear at the beginning what family rules are important, so that Granny or Grandpa understands too – but try to keep the rules simple and confine them to issues that really matter. It is easy for old people, not just children, to get confused about a lot of petty dos and don'ts.

If your own standards of courtesy and consideration towards your parent are high, there should be no behavioural problems in your children, but sometimes in adolescence children go through bad patches and you may find their behaviour towards your parent as well as towards you is rough and inconsiderate. Pat, whose grandmother lived with her family for several years when she was a child, recalls the shame she still feels about her fits of bad temper. 'I'll never forgive myself for some of the bad behaviour I showed to Granny. I wouldn't walk slowly with her – and she really couldn't hurry because of her bad heart. And once I threw a bunch of keys which hit her – I can still see her face. She wasn't cross, only sad. Yet

I was very, very fond of her and we used to spend hours going through the "treasures" in her chest of drawers: lovely boxes of lace, and little pieces of jewellery which we both liked (my own mother never cared for jewellery). I wish I could tell her now how much she meant to me.' Keep a weather eye on how your children conduct themselves and if necessary have a quiet word with them at a time when they are receptive – the odds are that they will thank you when they are older.

MOTHERS AND DAUGHTERS (OR DAUGHTERS-IN-LAW)

This is the most common combination in one-home family relationships as there are more widows left on their own than there are widowers. In many ways it is easier to fit an elderly mother into the household than it is a father. She will tend to relate more to the children and be used to filling her time with small domestic tasks and to adapting to other people.

But be prepared for a time of adjustment, especially if your relative has just lost a husband and sold up her home. Familiar surroundings and possessions and the routine of visiting well-known shops and social clubs give that sense of security and identity so important to all of us, and with these taken away she is bound to feel disorientated for some time. So would we, despite the fact that we are younger and more adaptable.

If you are working, it would be wise, if it could be arranged, to take a couple of days off to settle her in. If this is impossible, try to arrange for her to come at a weekend, or arrange an earlier weekend visit so that you can go out with her with the express idea of showing her where the library, parks, old people's clubs, best shops, cafés and so on are sited. Of course, she will have visited you before and probably knows the neighbourhood, but it will be a very different matter for her to begin regarding it as her own home and district. If she has links with a church, chapel or synagogue it would be a good idea, even if you are not a churchgoer yourself, to invite the local vicar, deaconess or rabbi to visit for a cup of coffee early on in your mother's stay. At church or church functions she will certainly meet some congenial people.

Obviously you will want her to entertain her own friends and go out to meet them, so do make this clear from the start. This would also be the right time to raise the subject of your own and your children's social life. On no account should you give it up or cease to entertain your own friends or you will end up resenting the curtailment of freedom that your parent has imposed. It is also the time to indicate tactfully that you would appreciate a little time with your husband in the evenings on your own – perhaps to discuss a family problem, exchange information on what has been going on at work, or just relax alone. She might like to watch a favourite TV programme or listen to the radio in her room, or invite a friend in for a couple of hours to chat. She would probably appreciate a little privacy herself, but unless you make it clear that this is fine with you she might feel she is being unsociable if she goes off on her own.

Another thing to discuss at the outset is the matter of holidays. Arrangements can be made so that you can go off with your own family and friends for a complete break, and you should aim from the outset to do this. Find out whether there is another member of the family or one of her friends with whom she can stay – or perhaps a friend could stay with her in your home while you are away. She might, if handicapped or disabled, agree to go into a residential home for the time you are away and this should be discussed and arranged at an early stage.

You will probably have discussed financial matters before your relative moved in and have come to an arrangement about your mother's contribution to household funds. Obviously she will want to pay a basic amount towards food, heating and other household expenses and you will take account of what resources she has so that the amount is fair but still leaves her some of her own spending money. If from time to time she buys a small treat for the family, accept it graciously and never say, 'Oh, you shouldn't – you know you can't afford it!' – even if you feel the money would have been better spent on household necessities. It will mean a lot to her.

The matters so far discussed have been of a practical nature, and practical problems, on the whole, have practical solutions. Relationships, however, tend to be much more difficult. Usually a mother/daughter relationship is one of the easiest, although problems can arise if the parent is particularly domineering or given to emotional blackmail, or if the daughter is bossy and managing. The latter may be so if she is at work and has too much to do, combining a job, running a home and family and now caring for a parent, who may have some disability as well. The mere task of getting through everything may make her say 'Do this, do that' though she does not mean to be dictatorial. If you feel this is your problem, it will pay to be frank with your mother and your family and explain why. It would do no harm to ask for help and co-operation from everyone else as far as they are able to give it; they simply may not have realized how much you were doing.

By enlisting your mother's help as woman to woman, you will make her feel useful and not a burden, and the bond arising should help to strengthen the relationship. Perhaps she could peel vegetables for the evening meal or be responsible, if she is in, for giving the children tea when they come back from school. If your mother is the bossy one, and says, 'Now let me do such and such', don't feel you are giving up the reins of the household by accepting help. She may long to feel useful and show that she is competent, even though she is elderly. After all, she has run her own household for a very long time. Accept the help with thanks, but tell her that if it ever becomes too much for her you will understand.

It is often difficult to change the parent/child relationship and the attitude 'Mother knows best' is a very hard one to shift. It need not matter too much if mother and daughter have their own separate households, though very often there can be disagreements when grandchildren come along and mother and daughter have diametrically opposed views on such subjects as, for example, potty-training. But of course when mother and daughter are in the same house, the problem can become acute and the relationship, to succeed at all, will have to be put on a different footing. The women will need to relate to each other as two individuals and be tolerant of each other's foibles, just as friends would be. In the case of parent and child, mutual love and shared memories can be a help in getting over the personality clashes which may well occur in the first weeks of adjustment. Without being pushed too much, the parent should be encouraged to develop outside interests or take up the threads of an old hobby which she used to enjoy. If she is strong and well enough, there is plenty of voluntary work in which she could be involved. She need not be with old people in this capacity if she does not want to be: many organizations would be delighted to welcome a 'granny helper'; in a playgroup, for example, she could read to the children or make refreshments. Having outside interests to talk about within the family is a great prolonger of youthfulness.

Always remember that the odds are stacked in your favour. You have your partner and family and your own home. You have someone to have a quiet grumble to when things get tough – which brings me to the man in the family. Despite music-hall jokes about the husband's mother-in-law, there are many in-laws who get on very well together, can share jokes and enjoy one another's company. If, however, your mother is critical of the man you have married or are living with and compares him unfavourably with her late husband, because of what he either does or does not do, you will have to redress the balance and point out the things in his favour, even gently reminding her that your late father was not perfect either. It is a mistake to become too defensive – although you may want to – as this is likely to harden her attitude, but if she gets to know him better, through you, in a relaxed atmosphere, you can hope for matters to improve.

If you are looking after a mother-in-law, the situation will be slightly different. You may get on very well together, but there are different snags to look out for and to smooth out if necessary. It might be difficult sometimes, for example, not to resent all the work you are having to do for your partner's mother and to feel that he is not pulling his weight and should be doing more. And you may feel that you are neglecting visiting your own father and mother as you have less time. Your mother-in-law may feel jealous of you in relation to her son – many women feel far more possessive about their sons than they do about their daughters – and may keep reminding you of incidents in his boyhood and how fond he was of her when he was a lad.

Try not to be too possessive yourself and make opportunities for your husband to talk to his mother alone, to
take her out sometimes and to see that the suggestion
often comes from him to include her in family treats. Or if
he does this anyway, try not to resent it. He probably feels
it is up to him to make up as far as possible for the loss of
his father and it may not occur to him at all that you might
feel your own relationship with him is threatened (which
of course it is not).

You may well resent criticism and interference from
your mother-in-law more than from your own mother,
and if this looks like being a problem at the outset (after
all, you will have known her before she moved in with
you) it will pay to be polite but firm and let her know that
as you would not expect to interfere with her way of
doing things, her family and her friends, neither would
you expect any interference from her with the running of
your home. If she is particularly strong-willed and dominant and you find you are becoming the same, clashes of
personality will be inevitable at some stage, so it will be
even more important to encourage outside interests as an
outlet for her energies. She may be a very good organizer,
in which case her capabilities would be appreciated by
some organization in which she was interested. If she is
largely confined to the home owing to disability, the
situation will be more difficult, but it may be possible for
a volunteer to bring in work for her to do there (perhaps
putting circulars into envelopes or some knitting or
sewing to be sold for fund-raising).

Taking an objective look at the situation, you may be
surprised to find that if she is a difficult mother-in-law,
you are being a difficult daughter-in-law. A good laugh
together over this would probably clear the air.

FATHER OR FATHER-IN-LAW
More rarely it is the father or father-in-law who is taken
into the family home. Much of what has been said about
female parents will naturally apply to fathers also. In
many cases it is more difficult to persuade a father to leave
his own home and come to live with his offspring, even
though he may be finding the practical problems of
looking after himself overwhelming.

Jane's father, for example, lived over two hundred miles away from Jane and her family, and as she had two very small children visiting was difficult, especially as she had no car. Her father had a good offer for his bungalow, and when he came to stay with Jane in London they found a small modern flat fifteen minutes' walk from where she lived. It was agreed that the sale of the one and the purchase of the other should be made as soon as possible. Jane had a part-time job and an *au pair* girl, and it seemed a good idea for her father to spend plenty of time in her house with the children, especially as the *au pair* would get his meals when Jane was at work.

'It all seemed settled,' said Jane, 'then one evening we had a phone call from Dad saying that he couldn't face uprooting himself, didn't like London and as I was working and wouldn't give up my job (I couldn't give it up for financial reasons) he really didn't think he'd see enough of me to make the move worth while. My heart sank. He wasn't very well, and we (including the kids) had been looking forward to having him near where we could keep an unobtrusive eye on him. I only worked two days a week, so there would have been plenty of time for him, but I felt I couldn't be emotionally blackmailed into giving up my job.

'I also knew that the one thing he hadn't said was that my mother was buried in Cornwall and he didn't want to leave her – irrational as that might seem. So we had to let his decision stand. In fact, he made a very good job of looking after himself, with the help of some kindly young neighbours, but in the end they moved away. He had a stroke four years later and we had to rush down there, all of us, and he died in hospital after a short illness. I still feel I should have done more to persuade him to live with us. There would have been problems as he and I never hit it off as well as my mother and I had, but we would I'm sure have got on better after a time and the children would have had some happy memories of one grand-parent – they were too young to remember any of the others.'

It can be very difficult to know how to persuade a reluctant parent to come and live with you. The final decision must be his or hers, unless increasing infirmity has made a change of lifestyle essential. If you take a male parent into your home you will probably find, unless he is unusually domesticated or has been used to doing the housework for an invalid wife, he will not interfere in the cooking or in the way you run the house. However, he will probably follow you round and want to talk, especially if he has not yet developed any of his own interests in your district or made any new friends. And he may demand a great deal of running round and physical care, as he may have done from his wife.

He will probably appreciate as much company as your partner can give him when he is at home, and there may well be interests such as sport which they can share. Many men can find a basis of discussion and get on well, but your husband will not appreciate it if your father (or his own father) tries to lay down the law and make decisions which are rightly his or family ones. Thankfully not many of us are called upon to take an Alf Garnett into our homes, but if a man has been used to authority in a job and in his own house it can be very difficult to adjust to living somewhere where he has no automatic right to say what should or should not be done. This may, in fact, have been the basis of Jane's father's decision to remain where he was.

May, whose elderly blind father lived with her and her family (a husband who, she said, was 'very eccentric' himself, and three young children), had this point to make. 'When Mark and my father didn't get on or had an argument or disagreement, I made very sure that, however much I wanted to, I didn't interfere. This was after several experiences of being piggy-in-the-middle when I was nearly torn in pieces by conflicting emotions in myself and by my husband and father each trying to make me side with him.'

If there is some area in which your father can be in control and do as he wishes, it is to be encouraged. Perhaps he can do some decorating, or is good in the garden, where neither of you probably has much time to operate. If he is fit and active, there might be a small part-time venture he could organize – perhaps gardening or cutting grass for other people (it is usually very difficult to find anyone willing to put in just an hour or two a week and it could be a service very much appreciated locally), or doing those odd jobs that are always cropping up round a house and which many people are unable to do for themselves. Again there are organizations very eager for volunteers – the British Legion is one – or he might be able to find a part-time job which will give him company and a feeling of status. For men, particularly those of the older generation, status is often very important – something women generally find difficult to understand, as they can usually orientate themselves happily round family cares and interests.

Do not forget that a show of affection, warm and loving company and kindness are just as much appreciated by men as by women, nor that your father or father-in-law may be suffering greatly from depression and a sense of loss. The routine of work and the pattern of his own home life have gone, and while he may appreciate the freedom of retirement, it may help him if he establishes some new set patterns of life to give some form to his days. Many elderly people like to get up early, so if he would like to, perhaps he could bring your husband and you a cup of tea in bed as a luxurious start to the day. Maybe it could be his job to return library books once a week, and so on.

COPING ON YOUR OWN

Over 300,000 women in Britain today are responsible for caring for an elderly parent or parents. The problems they face are often very different from those which confront a family taking a parent into its home.

Perhaps one of the most difficult things to come to terms with is the fact that it is so commonly taken for granted that a daughter, either unmarried or perhaps separated or divorced, is the natural member of the family to take over responsibility when a father or mother is widowed or becomes too infirm to manage on his/her own. This should not be so, of course, but it usually seems to happen that she is obliged to make a judgement of Solomon: her decision either commits her to an unspecified number of years of caring or leaves her feeling guilty for 'opting out' if she puts the parent into residential care. Any woman of spirit might be forgiven for thinking, 'I will not slip into the slot which everyone else thinks I should occupy. I'll show them!' But love, loyalty and a sense of duty usually conspire to make her end up by shouldering the responsibility.

There may be a great conflict of emotions. Parent and daughter may be very fond of one another, but though the parent may be deeply upset at the thought of a beloved daughter being restricted and 'put upon' by his or her infirmity, no other arrangement may seem possible. If the relationship between parent and child is not so good, it may be that the new set-up is entered into with great reluctance – either party may feel that he is putting himself in a position of being dominated by the other. Unless great care is taken, parent and offspring may be thrown too much into each other's company, causing mannerisms and habits eventually to become a major source of irritation.

If the parent is not too infirm, the daughter will probably continue with her job. In this case, she will need all the help she can get both from professional and state organizations and from voluntary ones. In a sense, she faces the same problems as a woman with children – however exacting the job, concern for the parent or child at home will always be at the back of the mind; and what happens if the dependent person is ill? It is more acceptable in our society for a woman to stay away from work if a child is ill than it would be for her to do so because her mother or father is ill. There is the same necessity to rush home at the end of the day to face the domestic chores, however appropriate or useful it could be to stay and finish a piece of work, to stay behind for a chat with a colleague or to go out for a drink with friends.

In this one-to-one relationship, it is even more essential for the carer and the parent to preserve their own individuality and independence, for there is no husband and family to confide in, offer extra company or a safety valve for either side on a regular basis. The carer must make sure that it is understood by her parent that she must have time off, time to pursue her own activities and to meet or entertain her own friends. Obviously, too, the parent should have her own contacts and friends, and there should be mutual agreement on holidays and arrangements for her to have company or care at that time.

These psychological props of time off, company to look forward to and holidays are most important for both sides. If the parent seems to be becoming too possessive ('No one looks after me like Mary'; 'I don't know what I shall do when Ann goes on holiday'), the carer must harden her heart. If she does not have a break, she will not be able to go on doing her job, or looking after her parent, and her own health will suffer. All being well, however, she will not find herself coping with someone as difficult as Mrs Gibson in one of L. M. Montgomery's delightful *Anne of Green Gables* books. Mrs Gibson, who is 80, is looked after devotedly by her daughter, Pauline, who is never allowed a day off, let alone a holiday, by her selfish parent. Anne offers to look after Mrs Gibson for the day so that Pauline can go to her cousin's Silver Wedding party. All goes well until after Mrs Gibson's afternoon nap. Then, as L. M. Montgomery writes:

Nothing suited her. The drink Anne brought her was too cold; the next one wasn't cold enough. Of course, anything would do for her. Where was the dog? Misbehaving, no doubt. Her back ached. Her knees ached. Her head ached. Her breastbone ached. Nobody sympathized with her. Nobody knew what she went through. Her chair was too high. Her chair was too low. She wanted a shawl for her shoulders and an afghan for her knees and a cushion for her feet. And would Miss Shirley see where that awful draught was coming from? She could do with a cup of tea, but she didn't want to be a trouble to anyone, and she would soon be at rest in her grave. Maybe they might appreciate her when she was gone. "Be the day short or be the day long, at last it weareth to evening song." There were moments when Anne thought it never would; but it did.

There may come a point when a parent becomes so infirm that it will be a question either of putting her into residential care or of the carer giving up her job. This is a tremendously difficult decision to have to make. Unlike staying at home to have a baby and found a family, this is a situation with no built-in hope. It is inevitable that the older person will get worse rather than better, and there can be no future, only a past. To exchange a job in which one has had jolly company, exercised one's skills, made a contribution to an organization or firm, earned a salary and enjoyed an identity among other people, for the probably confined, confining and difficult task of looking after and nursing an elderly person indefinitely is very daunting. It is certainly a decision which merits plenty of thought and discussion, and not one the carer should come to on her own. If she has no family, or even if she has, a discussion with friends, a social worker or someone at an organization such as Age Concern should help to clarify her thoughts and enable her, with her parent, to come to the best possible decision. Not only are the emotional and physical responsibilities awesome, but if the carer gives up her job, in today's difficult employment situation, she may have problems in rejoining the labour force later on when she is free. And a drastic reduction in the amount of money coming into the house may have to be faced too. It may be that she can look forward to inheriting her parent's house eventually, but this is not always the case, and there may be a future to face with no job and nowhere to live.

An excellent organization for someone in this situation to contact is The National Council for Carers and their Elderly Dependants, mentioned earlier (address in Chapter 12). The Council will be able to give advice on both practical and emotional problems and point you in the direction of all the services and benefits you are entitled to from the state as well as putting you in contact with voluntary bodies which can help. One extremely valuable service for carers who will be without a home when their parent dies is help in planning future accommodation.

As far as local arrangements are concerned, if your parent is living with you it is essential to find a regular 'parentsitter' who will be congenial to your parent and can do everything necessary while you have time off. Perhaps you have a relative who is willing to help, or your mother has a younger and fitter friend who would like to be with her for a time. If money is short and you cannot pay someone to come, and you do not know of anyone who could fulfil this function, it is well worth contacting Age Concern to see whether a suitable volunteer can be found to help. Or you might be able to exchange babysitting on your part for parentsitting on someone else's, if you have young neighbours. It is obviously important to make sure that whoever you find is congenial to your parent before you make the arrangement long-standing. A cup of tea and a chat will usually help everyone to make up their minds.

When you start looking after your parent, it will pay to organize yourself as far as accommodation and funds will allow. If you are at work, a small freezer, microwave oven, dishwasher, washing machine and spin dryer (if you do not already have them) could be well worth buying for the time and energy they will save you. Having a good cook-in once a week would enable you to stock the freezer with individual meals which your parent could heat up for lunch in your absence or which could make a main meal for the two of you at night. Stack up several meals' worth of dishes in the dishwasher and forget the washing up – it works for families, so why not for you, your parent and your friends? Such aids are great morale-boosters.

Gillian, in her fifties and working full time as secretary to a group advertisement director in a big company, was, although suffering badly from rheumatoid arthritis, looking after her 90-year-old mother at home. Her mother had gone deaf, and Gillian found it necessary to dash home every lunch hour as well as immediately after work to look after her. As Gillian was there to provide one hot meal a day, her mother was not entitled to meals-on-wheels, and they were only allocated a home help for 1½ hours a week. 'Meals-on-wheels would have been a boon to me in the past,' says Gillian, 'but now my mother has to have all her food puréed, which I do with a fork and mouli, which takes ages. I try to work ahead and freeze some, but sometimes I don't have time in the evenings to have anything to eat myself. Then my mother gets worried. But extra catering like this is a lot more trouble than just cooking a meal for two.' This is where a food processor or blender would be helpful, as Gillian could cook enough food for two and purée her mother's portion very quickly. Living as she does in a London suburb, Gillian has, in the past, found the DHSS 'brilliant'. But now, she says, the staff has changed and the new people do a lot less. The DHSS blames the deterioration on financial cuts.

What is a reasonable amount of time for a carer to have off? To some extent this depends on circumstances, the health of the parent, financial resources, and so on, but some people consider that a month is not too much holiday to have (not necessarily away from home, unless cost is no object), probably divided into a spring and autumn week and a fortnight in summer. If your parent is in need of nursing, you may be able to arrange for her to go into hospital for a limited time for care, or, if money is not a consideration, she could enter a private nursing home or have nursing care at home. Organizations such as BREAK (see Chapter 12) can offer accommodation at certain times of year and are equipped to care for profoundly disabled guests.

CARING FOR BOTH PARENTS

Although in some ways it may be more difficult to look after both parents, in other ways it can be easier. If they are pretty fit, the advantages of their having each other's company and their long habit of being together, the fact that they can support each other, and do things to help each other, will take some of the work off the carer.

If they are both ill, the situation will be difficult. John and Joan lived in a modern bungalow with their large family, and John's old parents lived in a cottage next door. This arrangement worked well for many years. Joan took the old people shopping, to hospital appointments, to the hairdressers, and so on, but they were otherwise very independent. The father could still climb a ladder to fasten up a clematis in the summer after he was 90. Unfortunately, both parents were taken ill at the end of that summer. John's mother had had cancer and was suffering from Parkinson's disease. Gradually she became so frail that she could no longer cope. His father suffered a heart attack, and although both old people were very reluctant, they had to be moved into the bungalow. The spare room was given to the father, and the mother had a bed in the large communal sitting-room. Although both parents were very concerned about each other, they had disagreements when they met, largely because of difficulties over communication. They were both very deaf and neither could hear what the other was saying. John's mother became very confused and thought her daughter-in-law was leaving home although she had only gone away for a short holiday.

Family life was completely disrupted and the family were worn out with being up all night as the old lady needed constant care and had to be turned two or three times an hour. Eventually things got so bad (and in this case there was not too much help from the district nurse, who, instead of visiting every day, came once a week, at best) that the old lady had to go into hospital, much to her unhappiness, for the expert and continual nursing care that she needed. The father made a good recovery and was soon sitting up in a chair, then going over to see that everything was all right in the cottage. He visited his wife regularly, but she became even more confused, hitting and throwing things at him, which of course upset him terribly.

This family tried hard to do the very best for the old couple. Was there any other course of action they could have tried? Other members of the family (John's two sisters) rallied round, but like everyone hoped that the problem would just go away. It did not. John's father died suddenly of a heart attack; his wife had meanwhile been moved from hospital where, although not expected to survive for long, she recovered. There was no place for her in a state home or long-stay hospital so the family found her a place in a private home which offered nursing care. The cost was around £160 a week, far too much for the family to afford on an on-going basis, but the DHSS stepped in and paid most of it. It was very harrowing for all members of the family as she longed to get home again, although it would have been out of the question to provide adequate nursing care. She died still asking to come home.

This family had horrific problems, but no single carer could have coped with such a situation. Discussion with the local social worker and parents' GP could however have made it possible for the parents to have gone into residential care at a much earlier stage than John's mother did.

NANCY

'My mother-in-law used to live in the north of England, quite a long way from us,' said Nancy, 'and although her daughter lived quite close by, she hardly ever bothered to go and see her. Then she had a stroke and went into hospital, which was a great worry, and my husband and I decided that she would have to come and live with us when she came out. In fact, she made a very good recovery – 95 per cent physically and 100 per cent mentally – but we still thought she should come, looking ahead to possible further illness. The deciding factor was a very bad winter, when her daughter wouldn't have her and she was on her own, so we took it from there.'

As Nancy's bungalow would have been too small for her husband's mother in addition to herself, her husband and their son, they decided they would have to extend it. 'We felt that it was essential for us to have our privacy and for her to have hers for the operation to work at all,' she explained.

'I don't think many people know this,' she continued, 'but you can get a statutory grant for extending your home to accommodate a disabled person.

'You need a medical certificate, of course, and you can get up to 90 per cent of the cost if your home is judged to be too small for you to take your relative in. If you are in doubt about your home or qualifications for a grant, I'd recommend that you explore the possibilities. We got a grant of £8,000 and it turned out that we had to find another £4,000 of our own, but we were able to build on really good accommodation for her.

'If she goes away to live for any reason other than medical, we would of course have to repay the grant.'

I asked how the family felt about taking in Nancy's mother-in-law, and she told me: 'We were all quite excited about it, particularly when we were planning the accommodation for her. My husband kept saying "Mum will love this", whatever we were thinking about to make it nice. In fact it's all new and lovely, there isn't a thing you could think of that we haven't done.'

And how has it all worked out? Not quite as they expected, it seems. 'I never anticipated that things would be so hard,' said Nancy. 'Mum was always a difficult woman, though in fact after she first had the stroke she became much more easy-going. Unfortunately this mellow outlook didn't continue. Nothing we can do is good enough – she's contrary *about absolutely everything. Although her surroundings are so convenient, there's no pleasure in having her with us.*

'We've tried to give her lots to interest her, suggested hobbies and occupations, but we can't cheer her up. She doesn't want to knit, sew, watch TV or anything like that. She just sits all day. I'm normally a bright, optimistic, cheerful person and I'm very used to helping old people. There was a couple in our village who lived in really squalid conditions – you wouldn't believe the things I had to do for them – and they were always so cheerful and such fun to visit, especially the old man, who had a real twinkle in his eye. But Mum's attitude is getting me down. I'm working full time, so it's quite a lot of extra hard work too. I leave her meals in Thermos jugs so that she doesn't have to do a thing. And of course I do all the housework. I've arranged for her friends to pop in, and the priest, and she does go to a day centre from time to time. But I arrive at the office fagged out – it takes me at least half an hour to recover – and when I go home at night I can feel myself go tense as I walk up the path.

'I have insisted that Bill and I have our meals alone together and that we have our own family holidays (she has a sister who will come when we are away). I know she probably can't help it, that she's lonely and has been ill, but she really does seem to try to drive a wedge between Bill and me – perhaps it gives her a feeling of power. I think it's rather like a child who wants to test the people to whom he belongs to the utmost, to see just how much they will put up with. Fortunately, the situation seems just to have drawn Bill and me closer together, thank goodness.

'We don't get very much help. Application for an attendance allowance was turned down, and although we're supposed to get all but £3 of her pension, we don't – and of course we wouldn't insist. Heating is a nightmare – the bills have doubled since she came.'

Would Nancy do the same again, if the clock could be turned back?

'Well,' she said, 'she was basically a good mother, and I would feel we had to take her in. When the crunch comes, you really do look into your heart and whatever you decide, it's going to be hard. But I would have no conscience if she had to go into a home later on for medical reasons. You can only do the best you can, and you do have a duty to your family too.

'I don't feel hurt, I just feel detached. However, I'm very sorry for my husband, who feels very badly about the whole thing, particularly from my point of view.

'But you just have to go on from day to day. The old saying is certainly true – that bread and water and a cheerful spirit are much to be preferred to rich living and complaining. I still remember my own grandmother, who lived with us when I was a child. She was originally very rich, but when her husband died the crash came and she was left with nothing. She decided to go on living in the grand manner and took housekeeping posts in very wealthy families, only retiring at the age of 82 when she came to live with us. She was a splendid character – as a child I had to make an "appointment" to talk to her, and she taught me lots of things like how to lay the table so that it was absolutely right. She was lovely to talk to and when she died at 86, the whole family missed her. I'd like to think people thought that about me when I died. I don't think old people are necessarily a nuisance. Getting along together is all about attitudes of mind.'

CHAPTER 6

Day-to-day problems

Many doctors nowadays are trying to prescribe fewer drugs for elderly people, particularly as some tend to have unwelcome side-effects, perhaps because the organs of absorption and elimination in old people do not always work as efficiently as they should, which can cause a build-up of the drug within the body. However, for many old people medicines are a necessary part of their lives and are keeping them going.

Unfortunately, it is an inescapable fact that as we get older, the minutiae of life become more and more difficult to cope with. Forgetfulness can strike us at any age, and we all know that if medication has to be taken at regular times it is only too easy to forget whether we have done so or not. With, for example, eyedrops which may need applying six times a day to control glaucoma, it is not only difficult to remember when they have to be put in, but very easy to forget whether you have done so. And with such items as sleeping pills, forgetfulness can be downright dangerous. It may be, too, that your parent has to take several different kinds of tablet, which can lead to even more confusion and difficulty.

If your parent is living with you, you will be able to ensure that she only takes the prescribed quantity of medicine during any one day, though it is better not to take the administration of her medicine completely away if it can be avoided. The more independence she can retain, the better from every point of view. However, even if she is living on her own, there are ways you can help her keep a check and make life easier for herself and less worrying for you both.

She will probably have a medicine cabinet in the bathroom, but if not, or if it seems better to keep the drugs separately, encourage her to put aside a shelf for medicines. It will be much easier for her to see what is there, when anything needs renewing and generally keep tabs on them than if they were kept in a drawer. Failing that, a small high-sided tray could be used, conveniently situated.

Labels and containers for medication often prove stumbling blocks for old people. Some labels are printed in tiny print, often on a coloured background, or are illegibly written so that even a younger person with good eyesight will have difficulty in reading them. It is essential that your parent can read what each packet or bottle contains, what the dosage is and how frequent, and whether the medication should be taken before, with or after food. It should be possible to arrange with your relative's doctor or pharmacist, or the district nurse if she is visiting, to have special large-print labels or tags to solve this problem. There is also the matter of opening the containers. While children seem to have little trouble in breaking into supposedly child-proof containers (as has been shown on television), older people frequently find it difficult to get their bottles and containers open, either because their fingers are weak or they have arthritic hands, or because they cannot see the arrows which have to be lined up, or the instructions on how to open the bottle are unclear – or for some other reason. A young friend recently brought round a bottle containing pills he had been prescribed and challenged us all to open it. No one managed it! If this is a problem, ask the pharmacist to provide bottles with special tops which are easier to cope with.

If you can visit frequently, you should discreetly check on what is on your relative's medicine shelf, having made sure you know what is being prescribed and what proprietary medication your parent is taking. Anything out of date or left over from a previous complaint should be flushed down the lavatory, but if a course of tablets has been prescribed and has not been finished by the due date, check with the doctor. If you live at a distance, enlist the help of a friend or neighbour, nurse or home help – someone who sees your parent regularly – to keep a check.

If your parent has to take several different kinds of medication, some long-term, some short-term, she may well appreciate having some kind of chart made and pinned up next to the medicine shelf so that she can mark off what she has taken. The chart can have sections to record the medicine, what it is for, the dosage and the times it has to be taken, together with columns for the days of the week, with room to tick off each pill or dose as it is taken. Having designed the chart, you might wish to get it photocopied and date one copy for each week covering the next few weeks, ready to fill in. She may need your help at first in filling in the chart. If she has a lot of problems and you are not there much, again enlist the help of someone who goes in regularly.

If you can visit, say, weekly, it might be helpful to sort out a week's pills, put out in separate containers (matchboxes, perhaps, or the little glass bottles in which herbs are sold) labelled for each day of the week and with the time to be taken on each. Special boxes, divided into sections, are available from chemists, but as with the first method, it is important, unless your parent is exceptionally clear-headed, that she has help in working the system and that there is a check to make sure she is taking the right medication at the right time. This will certainly make it easier for her and you, or whoever is keeping an eye on her to see if there is a problem, otherwise you will have to have complicated count-ups of pills from time to time to work out whether too few or too many have been taken.

Whenever possible, check with your parent's doctor or district nurse to see whether any particular drug prescribed has side-effects. The ones which might be expected may not, in fact, occur, but it is better to be aware that they might rather than be alarmed if your parent suffers, for example, recurring dizziness or headaches, or even constipation or vomiting. Doctors rarely mention side-effects unless directly asked about them. Check too that there will be no reaction with the drug if, say, your parent has alcohol, or that it will not react with any proprietary medicine she may be in the habit of buying. It will also be useful if you can understand how the prescribed drug can be expected to help your parent's condition.

If your parent seems to be addicted to proprietary medicines and is in the habit of buying and using them regularly, this again is something to check with her doctor. Certain products can have undesirable side-effects, just as some prescribed medicines can, and most people are not aware of these. I did not realize, for example, until an elderly friend had to be taken to hospital with severe stomach problems, that aspirins, which he took regularly as pain-killers for rheumatism, can cause bleeding and irritation of the stomach lining, which can be quite serious in some people. Some laxatives, which many old people take in quantity as they become very worried about constipation, can dehydrate the user; it is far better to encourage the eating of fibre in the diet (fruit, vegetables, cereals high in fibre) and as much exercise as possible instead. Some cold remedies contain agents for drying up mucus which can adversely affect glaucoma sufferers, so again, do check whether the proprietary medicine could exacerbate an existing medical condition. Occasionally one can be alerted by enlightened manufacturers. Recently a friend with glaucoma told me that there was a warning on a bottle of travel sickness tablets against taking them if you suffered from this eye problem. But on the whole such warnings are all too rare.

If a new drug is prescribed, either in addition to or instead of one that is currently being taken, this can also cause confusion and break an established pattern of pill-taking. It is very important to sort out what has been dropped and what added, and establish the new drug as carefully as possible, making sure that the drugs which are retained are still being taken at the right time and in the right quantities. If your parent has been in hospital and returns home, she may bring new prescriptions back and be confused as to whether she has to keep on taking the ones she was formerly using at home and of which she may still have a supply. In hospital she will have been given her medication at the right times and in the right quantity by a nurse, so she will not have been used to dealing with it herself. It is important to make sure both such situations are properly managed.

If you are living some way from your parent and are worried about her medication regime, you could arrange to phone at a certain time of the day to make sure that she has remembered to take her medication. Not only will your call act as a reminder, but she will welcome the opportunity for a short chat.

Not all problems, however, are connected with the taking of pills and medicines. There are many small things which can make all the difference to comfort and a feeling of independence, particularly if your parent is living on her own. As has already been mentioned, some people experience difficulty in dressing, perhaps because of a rheumatic condition or increasing physical weakness. Clothes that are easy to put on and fasten, perhaps a pick-up stick to help with putting on stockings and a stick to pull up shoulder straps, and choosing slip-on rather than laced or fastened shoes, can all help. Your parent may prefer to have her comfortable pair of shoes repaired rather than trying to 'break in' a new pair of shoes. Other simple gadgets include aids for men to put on their socks, or jackets, for example. The Red Cross's catalogue *Aids for Disabled People* would be worth consulting even if your parent is only mildly unable to cope. The Disabled Living Foundation (see Chapter 12) also has a clothing adviser whom you can consult on all aspects of clothing.

An occupational therapist will give good advice on which aids would be most useful for your parent, and she will also help to suggest new techniques for doing things such as putting on a sweater or shirt if, for instance, one arm is immobilized.

Your parent will almost certainly use spectacles, at least for reading, and it is very important to make sure that she does not forget to have a regular check-up, about every two years. She should also tell you or her GP if her sight begins markedly to deteriorate: this needs expert help. If new glasses are needed and your parent cannot afford them, she should ask the optician for a form to fill in and send to the DHSS. Make sure that the house your parent lives in is adequately lit; replace 40-watt bulbs with stronger ones where necessary (check that the shades are suitable for taking the stronger bulb; if not, replace these too). This could make all the difference first to safety and then to your parent's ability to read easily. A good magnifying glass could also be a help to some people – check with the Disabled Living Foundation for types available.

Many elderly people lose their acuteness of hearing with time, even if they are not completely deaf. As this can cause isolation as well as inconvenience and sometimes danger, it is essential to persuade your relative to be tested and fitted with a hearing aid if necessary. Sometimes the deafness is partly caused or aggravated by wax in the ears – a condition to which the hearing aid itself can contribute. The doctor can syringe the ear; otherwise, a good proprietary product that dissolves wax can be bought from the chemist. (See Chapter 9.)

In order for your parent to keep fit, she must be able to eat properly, so care of the teeth should not be neglected. If she has some natural teeth, they should be regularly inspected and cared for; it is better that major dental work such as the pulling of teeth and provision of dentures (if none have been worn before) should not be done when a person is old. Regular brushing of natural teeth and the cleaning of dentures if worn are essential for the health of the mouth. Teeth should be cleaned by brushing from the gums downwards in the upper jaw and *vice versa* for the lower one.

About 80 per cent of people over 55 have no teeth of their own, and if dentures are worn they should also be regularly inspected and checked for fit. Badly fitting dentures can cause problems with the mastication and digestion of food, and can also cause sore gums. Easy-to-eat foods such as bread and cakes may be preferred by those who find it difficult to eat more 'chewy' foods, but this can cause an imbalance in the diet. More resistant foods can be minced or liquidized, and although this may make them rather less appetizing, it will ensure a more balanced diet. Having good dentures or natural teeth is certainly better for morale and for the appearance of the face; there is no doubt that people with no teeth tend to 'age' more quickly in the face.

An elderly person with some teeth of her own should visit her dentist every six or twelve months, and if she has dentures these should be inspected every four or five years. If there are problems over tooth-brushing, such as difficulty in holding the brush, it may be possible to adapt it by making the handle more bulky so that it is easier to hold.

Foot comfort is also an essential part of keeping fit and mobile in later life. Comfortable shoes, rather than down-at-heel slippers, should be worn and the legs should be warmly but not tightly covered.

Regular foot care by a chiropodist is desirable, but chiropodists are in short supply, at least within the social services; however, if they *are* available home visits can be arranged. Private chiropody is also available (see Chapter 12). Any problems such as corns or difficult nails should be dealt with, ideally by a chiropodist, and if your parent has poor circulation or diabetes you or another carer should do the routine task of cutting her toenails for her – if she cut her toe it could quickly lead to serious infection. Washing (in warm, not hot, water), carefully drying and powdering the feet every day can contribute greatly to foot comfort. Care should be taken to handle the feet gently and particular attention should be paid to drying between the toes. Clean the nails with a brush and see that nails are cut straight across. If the skin is very dry and brittle, a little oil or lanolin can be rubbed in.

One of the main problems in getting some elderly people to look after themselves properly is lack of motivation. It is only too easy not to bother to go to the dentist regularly, have an eye test, keep shoes in good repair and cut toenails if you are living on your own, as anybody will realize who has been alone for just a few days. Standards slip, as there is no one else to bother about. If you and your parent or your parent and a friend can go together to keep appointments, visit the shop for new shoes or shop for clothes, he or she will find it much more enjoyable and worth doing. After Jane's mother's death, she found that her father seemed to be quite incapable of buying new clothes for himself when he needed them; it emerged that he had always gone with his wife and she had had the final word on what he bought. When Jane accompanied him, he cheered up enormously and took far more interest in his appearance after she had given him her advice on what to wear.

A common day-to-day problem which your parent may be reluctant to discuss is difficulty in getting to and using the lavatory. While your parent may not actually be incontinent, he may not be able to get to the lavatory very quickly, perhaps because he finds it difficult to get out of his chair, because he has to go upstairs or because the seat of the lavatory is too low – and all this may add up to some distress, anxiety and discomfort. Raising his favourite chair on blocks, or even providing a couple of cushions in the chair, would ensure that he sits higher and might then find it easier to stand up quickly. Raised toilet seats are available to fit over most toilet pedestals or seats. They are plastic and washable and can make sitting down on the lavatory and standing up again very much easier. If the lavatory is upstairs and your parent has problems in getting up and down easily, it might be best to provide a commode chair for use downstairs during the day. There are designs available which look just like ordinary armchairs, so there need be no cause for embarrassment.

One or two simple aids for the bathroom will help to make bathing more comfortable for your parent. A rail to help him pull himself up is one possibility; a bath seat is another. Slipperiness of the floor of the bath can be a problem, and a non-slip rubber mat is a cheap and easy way to deal with this. If he has difficulty turning the taps on and off, special handles can be fitted to make it easier. Make sure that towel, soap and talcum powder are all within easy reach and that the bathroom heater is both safe and adequate.

Your parent will have a greater feeling of security, particularly if he or she is suddenly coping with life alone, if you check on his/her house and make sure that the locks on doors and windows are effective (but possible for the occupant to manage without difficulty). It might be well worth installing a peephole fitting in the door so that she can see callers before she opens it, and a chain on the door. Encourage her to give a trusted neighbour a key, so that if she goes out and forgets her own she can get in without difficulty (it is better to put it this way rather than saying it is in case of emergency). Burglar alarm systems are expensive, but if she can afford it and is nervous, it could be worth having one installed.

MAY

*'It's not just a question of a roof over their heads – it's giving
them a home.'*

This was the thought that remained with me after talking to
May, now a middle-aged widow, about her experiences as a
young wife when she took over the care of her blind father.
Her mother had been looking after her father, but the work
and stress involved had told on her and she had had a stroke
from which she died.

May and her husband Mark, who was himself far from well,
had just moved into a large house with their three small
children, all under six (the youngest was a new baby). The fact
that they had plenty of room, after living in a tiny house,
made May say to her husband, 'What do you think about
asking Father to come and live with us?' Her husband had
replied, 'Of course. We say we are Christians, so we can't do
anything else.' That was all that was said on the subject and it
was arranged for May's father to move in.

'The day he came was the worst day of my life,' said May.
'He had always been a very strong, autocratic man, head of
the family when we were children, and the house was
completely ruled and dominated by his moods. I could see the
same thing happening in my house, with problems arising
with Mark who was himself very eccentric.

'He always did what he wanted to do, with varying
disasters and problems. Although he was blind, he would go
out on his own, frequently falling off the kerb and once down
on to a railway line. To keep in touch, he used to go to a club
he belonged to by bus, and very often my mother used to have
to wait for him at the bus stop at two in the morning, in order
to make sure he got home all right (the buses used to run that
late in those days).

'He was a meticulous man and he even used to arrange the
coal in the cellar into graded sizes! His own house was always
dauntingly tidy. In a way this was good, when he went blind –
you may not realize, but you have to keep a very ordered and
tidy place if you have a blind person living with you, and to
remember such things as always shutting doors so that they
don't walk into them – my children soon got used to doing this,
and picking their toys up off the floor, too.'

I asked May how her father fitted into the household at
first, and whether her early fears were realized.

'In our house,' she said, 'no one ever quarrelled and no one talked about money. We always avoided conflict in our marriage and with the children, and as a result my father's personality changed considerably over the fifteen years he lived with us. He had nothing to fight about, you see, so he became less argumentative. Happily he and Mark got on very well on the whole, although when there were arguments I learned to keep out of the way and let them resolve them themselves.

'We all had our meals together (my father's food all had to be cut up for him) and he was very critical of the children's behaviour and was always telling them to sit down and be quiet. Eventually he asked if he could have his lunch in his own room if it wouldn't be too much trouble for me. So we organized it that he could eat there and just have his evening meal alone with Mark and myself. In the end he preferred to have this meal by himself, too, as he liked to listen to programmes on the radio which were not to our taste.

'He was a difficult man – he had always been very critical, and that didn't change. He couldn't do anything in the house, of course, and although Mark did help with the washing up, he was otherwise totally impractical and couldn't even put up a shelf, so I had to do all that side of it. My father liked his food – a cooked meal for lunch and a different one for dinner, so it was quite hard work. However, I felt it was all a matter of organization, so I'd do a grill for one meal with a sponge pudding, for instance, and at the same time put in a casserole for the evening and have a simple pudding such as tinned fruit and custard. I only once in all the fifteen years really lost my temper and blew my top, but I can truly say that tiredness went with me everywhere like a constant companion. I was so exhausted that when I eventually went to bed every night I felt as if I could fall through a hole in the mattress, I was so heavy with sleep. I remember telling Mark I'd like to take off my legs and put them in a bucket of water to cool down at night!

'There were moments of humour, though. At one of the most tiring periods when the children had been ill and my father had been especially trying, he asked me why I didn't learn ancient Greek!

'When Mark became seriously ill, I had to return to full-time work – not wanting to at all, but we needed the *money. I always remember coming home on a Friday night, when we'd have a meal of fish and chips from the fish shop, and driving past the side of the house. Through one window I could see my father with a glass of Guinness in his hand, his mouth opening and closing in conversation, through the next window I saw my brother visiting him and chatting, and through the next window I could see Mark sitting and reading. Never once did anyone think of setting the table, warming the plates and fetching the fish so that I could sit down to a meal. But that's just how they were. I know if it had gone on for long and I really felt I couldn't stand it any more, I'd have said something rather than letting resentment fester inside me.'*

I asked May if she had had to look after her father physically, but she said that he would rather have gone into hospital than let a member of the family wash, dress and physically care for him. Although he lived to be over 90, there was no mental deterioration. He wanted to dominate the life of the family, as do many old people, to give him self-respect and some power in the world. May found this very understandable. He was a very generous man, and contributed to the household budget from his small pensions and remained independent until his death. May herself never got any outside help of any sort, either financial or from the social services, but as she said, she did not apply – looking back, she thinks it would have been sensible.

The last few years were sad for May. Her husband became very seriously ill and had to go in and out of hospital for treatment. He died suddenly and unexpectedly in bed beside her. Her father, who never got over Mark's death, died soon afterwards.

'I came to like my father as well as love him,' said May. 'We both became less defensive as we lived together, and he always had a splendid sense of humour. Although tetchy, he had the capacity to laugh at himself as well as at situations, and we all learned to avoid the triggers which would set off an argument or emotional situation it would be difficult to get out of. Looking back, I'd say that this avoidance of problems by a little forethought and tact is one of the most important things in running a reasonably harmonious household containing several generations. The children always loved Grandpa and went to chat to him before they went to bed. But they had no illusions about him and I never encouraged them. If he was

difficult, we'd say so but try to remember "Well, he's old and blind". All my father's life and vitality came through the family – he had his routines, but as he lived to such a great age, one by one he lost his friends. The family was his stability and security. I could never go out without telling him what time I'd be back, and if I was ever late, he'd worry dreadfully, both over me and what would happen to him if anything happened to me.

'Another piece of advice I'd give to other carers is to be sure to have a holiday, at whatever cost in terms of making alternative arrangements. My father went to stay with my sister each year – it was not altogether successful from their point of view as they were too alike. The phone was always ringing as we got back to our house from the holiday, and it was my sister asking when we were going to collect my father. The other thing is, always give your parent a certain amount of time just to themselves with you each day – this sounds rather like the advice you give to parents about dealing with their children, but in fact it's rather the same.

'If you are in a situation like mine, you have to think of yourself as the fulcrum for the whole family – in my case, children, my handicapped father and my sick husband. You have to say to yourself, "Thank God I'm wanted and needed". After all, you could be, as so many people are, alone and unloved for years of your life. That would be so much worse than any amount of hard work.'

I asked May finally if she would blame a daughter in a similar situation who put her parent into a home.

'Emphatically not,' she said. 'I know that we could only make our arrangement work because we had the space and had just happened to move into a large house where my father could have his own territory and good big rooms to himself. If we had still been living in our previous small house, the arrangement couldn't possibly have worked. I would have found him a Catholic nursing or retirement home within visiting distance and made sure he was happy there. We can only do the best we can, and try to abolish guilt, which is destructive to all relationships.'

CHAPTER 7

Surviving stress: everyday relationships

However much you plan ahead in the business of caring for your parent, the stresses and tensions and the shifting patterns of personality interplay can be intensely wearing. Causes of stress can vary from such things as irritating mannerisms (sniffing, eating in a certain way, and so on) to 'penny-in-the-slot' reactions (mention Joe's house, and his mother always maintains that it is cold) and predictable turns of phrase (for example, those used in response to being asked to have something to eat or drink). These instances may seem very small and trivial in themselves, especially to someone not involved, but if you are tired or feeling a bit under the weather, they can irritate out of all proportion. Elizabeth and her elderly mother had a running battle over the use of Elizabeth's favourite small kitchen knife – a very sharp one which she always used in food preparation and had had for many years. Her mother persisted in using it, when Elizabeth was not around, to sharpen pencils, cut flowers and do other jobs round the house with it, in spite of being asked repeatedly to use some other knife or scissors. Ridiculous as it may seem to anyone who has not suffered similar irritations, that knife was nearly the cause of the whole mother/daughter relationship breaking up. One day the knife could not be found, and the mother insisted that she had not used it, but Elizabeth discovered it next morning when she went to clean out the solid fuel boiler – just the blade with the handle burned off. It had obviously been used to cut flowers, then thrown away with the newspaper and stalk trimmings. Many years after her mother's death, it still rankles with Elizabeth – 'She bought me another knife, but it was blunt. I'll always believe she threw mine away deliberately!'

Of course, your own reactions and habits may have just as grating an effect on your parent. And the same annoyances may also arise between an elderly husband and wife if one of them becomes deaf, forgetful or confused and the other finds this hard to take.

Your parent may be disabled or ill, depressed, lonely and missing her dead husband, may be trying to settle down in a strange place and regard it as home, and your natural feelings of sympathy may be struggling with impatience and also a feeling that, however hard it is for her, it is hard for you, too, with all the extra work and responsibility you, as carer, are involved in.

You may reach a point where you wonder how you can go on, not just because of the major demands made on you, but because of the continual minor stresses. Most of the challenges we face in life are stimulating: we feel that we undertake them for a good reason and that coping successfully with a new job, for instance, or pushing oneself to the limit in a sporting activity is a positive effort with a potentially beneficial outcome. The challenge of looking after an elderly and perhaps handicapped parent is in itself a tremendous one, and the rewards of making his or her life more comfortable, fulfilled and happier can be great, too, although the recipient of your care may not always appear to be grateful. What makes it harder is that the effort involved is a continual one, with no major goal to achieve; what is more, you are probably making that effort in isolation and with very little, if any, praise and commendation for anyone.

How much you can endure will depend on your own personality, your ability to relax and to cope with stress, and the amount of energy you have. Things which may not get some people down may, perhaps, be excessively trying to you – but remember that there will always be opposites and exceptions in this sort of situation.

Even if you are living in a comfortable home, have a caring family and money is not in short supply, you may still be feeling the pressures of full-time caring for your parent and be guiltily aware that they are getting you down. Even if you concede that it could be very much worse – for a single carer, for instance – your own burden remains the same. If you are in that situation, you may feel very keenly the lack of your old friends, your lack of freedom to go out when you wish, responsibility, fear of being ill and unable to cope, boredom, and petty arguments which can so often occur between people who are constantly in one another's company, whatever their ages. You may be feeling that you are on a treadmill from which you have no power to jump off. The thought of the end will probably also cause you anxiety and unhappiness – either because, despite your problems, you are very fond of your parent and will miss her when she dies, or because you feel guilty knowing what a relief it will be, however sorry you will be that she has gone. Not only that, but the thought of being the sole person responsible for nursing your parent through her last illness and attending her deathbed is a terrifying one, for you have to be feeling very strong and sure to resist the terrible power of death when you feel its presence in the room with you.

It may be possible to deal with some of the factors which are causing you stress and tension in a practical way. Other chapters deal with matters such as taking time off, sharing the responsibilities with other members of the family or outside helpers, meeting friends and encouraging your parent to see her own friends as much as possible. Many areas now have support groups and meetings for carers; such a group would be well worth joining, so check with your local Age Concern office to find out whether there is one nearby. Make sure you are getting as much help and support as is available from every source so that you are as physically rested as possible; exhaustion from lack of sleep can colour every aspect of your life, as Pam discovered (see her story, on pages 120–22).

Every situation is different, and every relationship is different, so there can be no universal panacea for winding down tension. Too many sleeping pills or tranquillizers, an increasing amount of alcohol, may do you more harm than good, but a release of tension can come from a good brisk walk or game of tennis, providing you have organized alternative care at home and are easy on that score. Meditation and yoga are now widely popular and many people find them helpful. Jocelyn took up meditation after the death of her husband, when she was trying to wean herself off the large doses of valium which she had started to take while nursing him through his long and painful last illness. It was a lifeline to her for nearly two years, until she returned to something like normal life. Yoga, too, where you 'breathe in strength and breathe out tensions and problems' and let any destructive thoughts that come into your mind flow away, is greatly relaxing.

Cultivating the right sort of attitude to stress may sound rather pompous, but in fact it can help enormously. First of all, upgrade your attitude to the job you are doing for your parent. Caring for a parent, another human being who may be helpless, is just as important as caring for an infant, and the work you do in the house and for that person means just as much. What you are doing deserves a high valuation, both in personal terms and in the context of society as a whole.

There are some lucky people who seem to be born able to find happiness and contentment in whatever role in life they are asked to play; you may not be one of them, but their attitude is worth cultivating and it is basically sound. Making the most of the present, getting out of it whatever it has to give, and feeling that everyone's role is important in the pattern of life can, if you really believe it, enrich your life and make what you do for your parent a positive rather than a negative part of your existence. This may sound an over-simplification, but you have sometimes to think of fundamentals, even if the reality of emptying bedpans, turning a bedridden parent, counting out his or her medication and administering it day after day can often seem thankless and never-ending.

Another help is to identify and deal with the causes of stress. At the beginning of the chapter some things which can drive people mad were mentioned. You can either face up to them, let them wash over you and laugh them off, or you can avoid them – perhaps by not providing the word or action that starts them off.

Henry's father, who was in his eighties, had lived for a long time in various parts of Africa when he was a young man. His attitude to society was extremely racist by today's standards, and with any suitable 'lead' he would launch into racially biased stories which infuriated his son and his daughter-in-law. This is a very obvious example, but Henry and his wife did eventually learn to avoid any possible word which might lead his father on to produce one of his stories (another factor was that he repeated the same stories *ad infinitum*, which made for further tension!). He had a fund of amusing and interesting facts which it was a pleasure to listen to, and by skilfully turning the conversation towards these, Henry was able to enjoy his father's company without pushing up his own blood pressure.

But as has been said, even very small and harmless mannerisms and habits can become a cause of stress in the carer (it must be said that Henry's father did not live with him all the time, so his stories were not a daily irritant). Drawing the sting from little remarks which can hurt or annoy is a knack which can only be acquired with practice, along with the awareness that often they are not intended to at all. If your parent complains, for example, that you have forgotten something you had promised to bring her, and this type of complaint gets out of hand, you can protect yourself by bringing out the old cliché, 'Yes, I'd forget my head if it was loose', rather than defending yourself by a long and loud and probably entirely justified account of how busy you have been that day and how many reasons you have for being forgetful.

It is always best to try to pass over or minimize disagreements over small matters, but there will be times when you should state and stand by your opinions. Do not feel that your parent should win the day all the time just because he or she is old and frail. There will be some issues which you will not agree over, and each of you has a right to your own opinion. It is not a good idea for either of your sakes to have loud arguments, but be quiet and firm when necessary and say what you believe.

Another great contributor to stress is the feeling, as previously described, that you are having to shoulder most of the burden alone (this can happen to carers living with their families as well as to carers on their own). Most of the people I have talked to have felt, very strongly, that the rest of the family have really not pulled their weight. This feeling very much applies to sisters talking about brothers in relation to the care of their parents. Typical remarks have been: 'It's all right for him – he's in South Africa, isn't he? He's always saying what a good life he could give Mum out there, but he'd have a fit if I packed her off on the next plane'; and 'My brothers are both married and live some way away, so my sister and I have to keep visiting Mother, doing her shopping and washing: I just don't think they realize how much we are having to do.' The general feeling is that they do too little and do it too late. By all means 'let off steam' to a friend, but try to preserve a calm and objective attitude to your family. A well-worded and well-reasoned appeal as to why you need some time off, or why it would be appreciated if they rallied round, should get you further than a harangue, however well justified it may be. If you are fond of your parent, you will not want to upset her if the family are divided and arguing because of her.

If you are living with your husband and family and looking after a parent or parent-in-law, you may feel that the other members of your family are not helping as much as they should do – this can cause tension particularly if it is a mother- or father-in-law you are having to work so hard for. A few days off for you or even a 'diplomatic migraine' could certainly help your family to realize how much work you are doing – just as, if you have a baby or toddler, leaving Dad to cope for a day can help to make him more aware of how much there is to do and how much his help is appreciated.

I have been presupposing that your relationship with your elderly relative is based on affection. Love, as they say, seasons all dishes. It can certainly help to reconcile you to many irritations and problems, as so many people I have talked to have found. If, however, the parent and the carer really do not get on and have no affection for one another, the situation becomes much more difficult. Jenny found herself in the position of having to care for her mother-in-law, who was as unwilling to move into Jenny's home as Jenny was to take her in. They had both fought against the situation, as they realized they were 'chalk and cheese' to each other, but no viable alternative existed. It took both of them a long time to accept the fact that Jenny would have to give her mother-in-law the 24-hour-a-day care she needed, and June, the mother-in-law, who had always vowed that she would never be a burden to her son and his wife, found it almost as difficult to accept the caring. Jenny resented the curtailment of her freedom – for the first few months she gave up most of her outside interests and regarded herself as a virtual prisoner – just as her mother-in-law did. In her case she was lucky. There was enough money to pay for some help to free her for the odd half day off and take care of the most irksome of the chores (her mother-in-law, because of her illness, was incontinent and could no nothing at all for herself). With time off and because her mother-in-law no longer felt herself to be an intolerable burden, they came to some sort of terms on which they could live together and respect each other, even if love was out of the question.

Sometimes it is not so easy. An elderly parent with an old-fashioned outlook on life and a disapproving tongue can find herself living with a daughter or daughter-in-law and her family (probably teenage children) whose per-missiveness she can only deplore day after day. Her disapproval probably causes worse behaviour from the teenagers, modern parents tending to overlook small misdemeanours in their children and saving the 'big guns' for totally unacceptable behaviour. The continual stress this puts on the carer who is in the unfortunate position of being in between the two protagonists is indeed difficult to cope with. The soap opera 'granny' who gives wise advice to grandchildren (we have seen it on *EastEnders* from time to time) does, of course, exist and many grandparents and grandchildren get on very well, but if this is not the case, diplomatic separation as far as possible would seem to be the only answer. Delia's mother, who lived with them, would try to answer the door if possible when student friends of her grand-children called, so that she could say, 'I'll see if he's in', shut the door in their faces and return muttering into the living-room saying, 'I don't know why he wants to come round – we don't want people like him here.'

Another problem is that of the parent-in-law (usually a mother) who tries to drive a wedge between her daughter and her husband. Delia's husband was working hard to build up his business when Delia's mother came to live with them. Fred often had to stay late entertaining clients, but however late he returned, his mother-in-law was waiting up to comment on the fact that he was very late, ask him where he had been and who he was with – with the implication that he had been up to no good.

All these irritations can add up to an enormous amount of stress and unhappily it seems to be elderly women who cause more trouble than elderly men. This is probably, on the face of it, because they have been used to living in a domestic situation and are still in one, but no longer in charge of events and the way things are run, so frustration causes interference wherever it can be applied. Men, on the other hand, do not worry too much about the way a house is run so long as they have company, conversation and are warm and comfortable. The fact is, too, that women survive longer than men, so that there is more variation in the experience of carers as far as they are concerned.

'It's all very well,' said Delia, 'advising people to make sure that they have their friends round and ask Mother or Mother-in-law to stay in her own room that evening. Mine never would, and she always grumbled to my guests over how badly she was treated and how unhappy she was – it got so embarrassing that in the end Fred and I just stopped inviting them round to our house. If someone won't co-operate, you can't force them to, and in the end I was just about at screaming point. But there was no way she would live on her own – she was happier tormenting us than being by herself. The only thing I would say is that she brought our family closer together than it has ever been!'

Another cause of tension can be the feeling that now the parent is elderly and helpless, roles have been reversed. The responsibility of the parent for the child has now been switched round and, however unwillingly, the daughter may find herself in the position of being Mother to an equally unwilling parent in the position of child. Alternatively, the parent may be in no fit state to realize that her life has to be organized by her daughter. It can be an emotional trap which the carer really does not want and can be difficult to come to terms with whatever the circumstances. A carer may have or have had her own children and feel her emotional needs as a parent fulfilled by them; she may therefore be unwilling to make parental-type decisions for her own mother or father. A

117

single woman, on the other hand, may not wish to lend herself to that type of emotional relationship, for which she may feel her lifestyle has not fitted her. Other carers may take over the role of 'parent' only too willingly, and not allow a parent to do anything for herself – which the parent may resent or accept so fully that she becomes less capable of helping herself than she should be. Some parents actually refer to their daughters as 'Mother'!

If this is a problem and a cause of stress to you, it is necessary to sit down quietly and look at the situation. There may be nothing you can do but accept it and try to relax as much as possible – it will depend on your parent's condition. She may always have been dependent, first on her own parents, then on her husband. Many elderly people have gone straight from living at home to getting married and living in a home with a partner, without any period of coping by themselves, and if a husband or wife has died, they may well feel the need to have a substitute on whom to depend. As May said, 'It is, after all, far better to be loved and needed, even if it is a tie for a time, than to have no one caring about you and to be emotionally isolated.' But if your parent is naturally independent, and you tend to be too 'managing', perhaps because you are so busy that this is the only way you can get through all the necessary chores, it will probably help you if you can allocate areas of responsibility so that your parent can feel she is in charge of at least part of her life.

You may be the kind of person who leaves the supper washing up until the next morning to do while cooking the breakfast, and this may drive your mother or father mad because they like to leave everything clean and tidy before they go to bed. So if your parent can do it, it could be one of his or her responsibilities to clear and wash up the supper dishes. This is a very obvious example; the situation may not be so clear-cut – particularly if your parent is incapable of helping, but quite capable of telling you how things should be done! However, it is your house, and the running of it is in your hands. If you quietly insist on this, it will have to be accepted in the long run.

More difficult to cope with was Delia's mother, who, when she first came to live with Delia and her family, insisted that she should do her share of the washing up, but the first three times she was carrying the tray of crockery to the kitchen dropped it and smashed the lot. After that she just told Delia when the washing up should be done and was excused the work herself.

Another difficult area is partisanship – especially that of an elderly mother for her son. She may 'baby' him and take his part against her daughter-in-law in a way that the daughter-in-law finds very difficult to accept (particularly if her husband rather enjoys it). The answer is probably to encourage the husband – or wife, if it is the other way round – to spend some time alone with his or her parent, go on an outing together or watch certain television programmes together so that the parent feels she is getting some of her offspring's time to herself. It will probably be found that if the husband has to go on business trips, his mother and his wife will get on much better. The biased-parent syndrome is not easy to cope with, but if husband and wife can talk about it calmly and sensibly and understand one another, this should help to avoid the worst of the stress.

Perhaps the best advice to carers on dealing with stress is to do something positive towards their future life, if time allows. If they are looking after their own children as well as a parent, they are, of course, already doing this. But a carer could, for example, think about a future career and go to evening classes, take a degree, study at home, improve a skill or get involved with some cause, either local or national. The challenge such a course presents will offset the stress of caring – a positive activity can often be more helpful than passive relaxation such as watching television. In other words, it could help more to play the violin (however badly) in an amateur orchestra than to listen to Yehudi Menuhin on records. Think of the old advice to stop sneezing: rub your wrist with an ice cube. It is quite a close analogy.

In addition to her duty towards and responsibility for her elderly parent, a carer also has a responsibility for herself, and although it may take a great effort to do so she should try to protect her own personality and interests for the time when her caring days are over.

PAM

For some carers help arrives too late, if it arrives at all. In Pam's case, her struggle to cope almost brought about a tragedy.

Pam and her husband ran a pub about a mile from where they lived, Pam doing all the cooking as well as helping in the bar. They were a successful and popular couple and everything was going well until Pam's father suddenly died. Her mother was left alone with Pam's slightly mentally handicapped sister, for whom she did everything and who was completely dependent on her.

Unfortunately Pam's mother's health started to deteriorate almost as soon as her husband died, and she began to exhibit signs of dementia, which grew rapidly worse.

'I began to notice pointers,' said Pam. 'For instance, she came down one day and said she had been talking to my Gran, who had been dead for twenty years. And once I went into the bathroom and found her washing the mirror in which her face was reflected, and not actually washing her face.'

It soon became clear to Pam that her mother and sister would have to come and live with her, her husband and grown-up son. Like many people, Pam had no experience of the illness from which her mother was suffering, and did not know what to expect. The classic symptoms quickly developed – wandering, waking every two hours and getting up ('We'd just get to bed about midnight after returning from our evening work in the pub, and then at one o'clock she would wake me up and call me so I'd have to get up and put her back to bed, and everyone else was disturbed, too.'), incontinence, complete forgetfulness of who her daughter and son-in-law were, and so on. Pam's husband was marvellously supportive, but her son threatened to leave home as he found the situation impossible to take.

'The pattern of my day went something like this,' said Pam. 'I'd get up at crack of dawn, wash and dress my mother and sister (often having to strip my mother's bed and change it, putting the soiled linen into the washing machine), give them their breakfast and do the housework, leaving them coffee and rolls for lunch. I hated doing it, but I had to lock them in so that I could go down to the pub and prepare the lunches for the customers. When I dashed back at two o'clock, my mother would be hammering on the door to be let out and I'd have to calm her down and try to give her and my sister some time before cooking their supper. They had to go to bed very early so that I could go to the pub and I had to lock the doors again. All the time I was working, I'd be worrying about the situation at home, and I found after a time I simply couldn't relax.'

I asked Pam if she had got all the help she could – a washing allowance, for instance, and other help from the local social services, but she replied that she did not know what help she could get as no one had told her. What about voluntary help – someone to sit with her mother and sister regularly, for instance? But she seemed to be quite unaware that such help existed. They tried hard to get her mother and sister into residential care (they could not be separated, which must have posed a problem) and the doctor was helpful with the applications, but each time they were turned down.

The doctor suggested giving her mother extra tranquillizers and sleeping pills so that Pam and her husband could get more sleep. 'But pills weren't the answer in our case,' said Pam. 'What I desperately needed was other people to help. Just to give us a break, an outing one evening a week, perhaps. We did have a home help for a limited time and she was good, but the hours she worked were very short.'

Eventually the family reached the limit. One night Pam swallowed an overdose of sleeping pills prescribed for her mother and was rushed into hospital. Her mother and sister were taken into care for the three days she was there ('for which we had to pay' said Pam, bitterly) and her husband ran the pub on his own. When she came out, the miracle happened – 'but it took an attempted suicide to do it' – her mother and sister were put into a residential home together; there, a little later, her mother died.

'My sister is a different woman now,' said Pam. 'She is not very severely handicapped and is quite capably helping the other residents, taking round meals, keeping them company. She's never been so happy, and it is quite clear that my mother did too much for her before. She would probably have had a far happier life if she had been encouraged to use her capabilities before. But my mother was too kind. She was a good mother, and I still feel I should have cared for her, but the nine months she lived with us literally nearly killed me. I think the social services in the area we lived in were very poor – but I probably didn't know how to make the right sort of fuss or *how to claim the help we were entitled to. I just rushed in and lived from day to day. I'd now advise anyone in the same position to find out what help they can claim and question anyone else they know.*

'It's nearly two years since my mother died, and I haven't really recovered yet, though I expect it will all fade in time.'

FRAN

When I rang up Fran, she told me she could not chat for long as they had Alan's widowed mother staying with them. This surprised me, as it was well after Christmas, and I thought Fran's mother-in-law had gone back to her own home in Dorset. Later, when I met Fran, she told me what had happened: it was a situation which could have ended in disaster, but this had happily been averted.

One afternoon at about four o'clock a neighbour of Alan's mother had phoned to say that the old lady was in the village shop in a very confused state, thinking she had been to the nearest large town on the bus, although it was not a day on which the bus visited the village, and altogether not making much sense.

She was living on her own in a centrally heated bungalow and was comfortably off, though she had her eccentricities. Among them was not ever having seen the doctor, although she and her husband had been registered with a local partnership when they first moved into the area over twenty years previously. Fran assured the neighbour, who was very diffident about having rung up, that she and Alan would drive down immediately. While waiting for him to arrive home from work, she phoned the doctor and received a promise that whatever time they arrived she, the doctor, would visit Alan's mother at her home; meanwhile the old lady was being cared for by the neighbour.

They finally arrived at about 8 pm and called in the doctor, who diagnosed Alan's mother as having incipient hypothermia (it was during a very cold spell at the end of February). She never liked to go out and leave the central heating on and apparently very often forgot to turn it on when she came in from shopping. Although in her case there was no need for major economies, like many old people she had long-standing habits of thrift and never used the central heating or electric fires unless she felt she had to.

In spite of all that had happened, it took Fran and Alan nearly three hours to persuade her to come back with them to their home and by the end, when she did eventually agree, they were nearly frantic with worry. (As it was, they forgot to turn off the water when they left, and when the thaw came the pipes burst.)

When they first saw Alan's mother she was terribly cold and her speech was slurred, but in her son's home she improved greatly after a few days of warmth and good food. The doctor said she had clearly not been eating enough, and Fran concentrated on building her up – in fact, she started to eat so well that Alan was worried that too much rich food (by her former eating standards) would be harmful. However, Fran saw that the improvement in her health brought about by good nutrition far outweighed any possible problems of indigestion.

When the old lady eventually returns home, Fran and Alan will continue to worry about her, because the factors which led up to her illness still exist. First, she lives a long way away from them, so there is no possibility of their popping in very regularly to check she is all right. She is a very self-sufficient woman and although the neighbours, as in most country places, are aware of how she is and that she is around, she does not encourage any friendships with them. There is only one village shop, which carries a limited stock, so she has to go by bus (she does not drive) to the nearest town to buy any delicacies or good convenience foods, and besides, she has not been very interested in preparing meals since her husband died. As she does not encourage the neighbours, they do not go to eat with her and have stopped inviting her to their houses as she never accepted in the past. Another major drawback to sorting her out nutritionally is that she will not consider having a refrigerator; she's been saying 'It's too late to bother' for the last ten years. Before that it was 'I'll think about it'. So there is no possibility of conserving food bought weekly in town. As she will not have a washing machine, she does all her washing by hand. Now, owing to arthritis, she finds it very difficult to stretch up and peg it out – and the local laundry service went long ago.

But the major worry factor for these long-distance carers is that she refuses to be on the phone. This is not a question of cost, but of old habits dying hard. Many old people are afraid

123

of using the phone, but for those who live far away from the people who love and care for them, a phone is an absolute necessity. Alan feels that he will have to insist on one being installed before his mother returns home. He will see that it is a phone specially adapted for people with arthritis in their hands, so that it will be easy to pick up.

Although Fran said she was worried at first that there would be personality problems during a long-term stay, the three of them are getting on well together and her mother-in-law is not difficult. She helps where she can, and is particularly enjoying doing some clearing up in the garden when the weather is fine. But she wants to return to her own home and at this stage it is still her decision. Fran and Alan will clearly have to make some plans for the next winter, not only for her sake but for their own peace of mind.

'There's no doubt,' says Fran, 'that eventually she will either have to come to live with us, or live in the area so that we can look after her easily. If, like us, you live in London, it is very important to talk to as many friends and neighbours as possible and benefit by their experiences. Boroughs vary so very much in what they have to offer the elderly. We are lucky in living in a borough which has excellent facilities and a great sense of responsibility as far as old people are concerned. But the one just over the border is quite the opposite, so if you were bringing an elderly relative to live nearby, rather than with you, and you had a choice, you would naturally opt for our area.'

CHAPTER 8

Financial and legal matters

This chapter will give some pointers to many of the benefits to which your parent may be entitled, from pensions to cheap bus or train fares, from national health prescriptions to false teeth. She may have her entitlements all well under control; on the other hand, she may not, so it is a good idea to know how to find out for yourself what she can claim, and what you, as carer, may be able to get as well.

Legal matters, too, should be considered at an early stage – see later advice in this chapter.

MONEY MATTERS

Indeed, money matters a great deal, not only to buy the comforts of life, but also for the reason that adequate financial provision in old age can contribute so much to your parent's peace of mind and to a feeling of independence. Not everyone, however, can provide for such financial reassurance and many retired people suffer a drop in income which, although expected, can still come as a great shock and be the cause of much anxiety and depression. Good budgeting is essential.

Most retired people will be able to plan their expenditure for themselves. After all, they know what their priorities are and how much they have been spending on such basics as heating, food, rates and the general running of their home. If, however, your parent (or parents) asks for help, first assess how much money will be available for expenses after any tax due has been paid. You may need to consult the Inland Revenue to find out how much tax, if any, will have to be paid on the income your parent will have from all sources (remember to add in income from investments as well as pension payments). If your parent has been working up to retirement and tax has been deducted by PAYE, he or she may find it confusing to try to assess what the new tax liabilities will be. Your best course of action would be to get all the figures together and make an appointment to see someone at the local tax office. The leaflets IR4, *Income Tax and Pensioners*, and IR4A, *Income Tax Age Allowance*, both obtainable from your tax office, will also be useful.

Once this has been done, it should be fairly simple to allocate a proportion to the major living requirements. Write down all expenses which have to be allowed for annually, such as rates, rent, heating, a budget for household repairs and repainting, any HP payments remaining, and insurances. These will obviously have to be revised annually as rates go up, or when HP payments end, and so forth.

Then basic living expenses such as food, household cleaning materials, shoe repairs, dry cleaning, soap, toothpaste, etc. should be calculated. It is helpful to keep an exact account for one or two months of this type of expenditure. Not only will this show how money is spent, but it may give a pointer to where economies can be made. It is important, incidentally, not to make the budget for food so low that your parent is missing out on a nutritious diet, but there will probably be ways in which he or she can save money by buying carefully and making sure there is no waste.

When the first two groups of expenditure are worked out, you will be able to see how much is left over for other items such as outings and entertainments, holidays, magazines and papers, TV rental, and so on. Some items will be difficult to assess: for instance, should a telephone go down as an essential, or a luxury or an optional extra? Depending on circumstances (where your parent lives in relation to your own home, and how well he or she is), it could be regarded as any of these.

As a report published by the BMA has said, 'Financial provision for elderly people should be sufficient to allow them to participate in social, cultural and leisure activities as well as to keep warm, fed, clothed and housed.' In other words, 'Man cannot live by bread alone': the quality of life people enjoy matters too. Unfortunately for very many old people, it is not even possible to keep warm in winter, let alone afford any luxuries. There is now growing pressure to change this state of affairs. As the same report observed, 'Elderly people are neither second-class citizens nor a race apart from society at large. They are equal and ordinary members of the community, and have a right to participate fully in the life of the community.' Planning expenditure can play an important part in ensuring that, even if resources are severely limited, they are disposed to the best advantage.

It may be that your parent asks you for advice on financial affairs generally, particularly if the parent is a widow who has not been used to filling in forms and dealing with household finances. One thinks of older women in this situation, but I know at least one woman in her late forties who is already dreading being left a widow later on, although her husband is still fit and active, as she has no idea how he handles their income and feels entirely unable to cope with any form-filling that may be necessary. Fortunately her daughter who lives nearby is very competent in such matters, so she will have help when or if the time comes.

You will, of course, persuade your parent that she should apply for every form of financial aid, or help in kind, to which she is entitled. A feeling still lingers in some of the elderly that they will be accepting 'charity' if they apply, for instance, to the DHSS. It will almost certainly be necessary for you to do some investigating and reading yourself to know what is due – no one is born knowing all the ways in which the state can help older people. Age Concern's inexpensive booklet *Your Rights for Pensioners* lists all the welfare benefits to which the elderly are entitled. It is obtainable at W.H. Smith, otherwise ask for it at your local Age Concern office or write to the address given in Chapter 12.

The following leaflets are available from the local social security office, or free of charge from DHSS Leaflets (see page 212):

FB.2 Which Benefit? A useful short summary of all the social security benefits.
FB.6 Retiring? This leaflet covers all aspects of the retirement pension together with information on supplementary pension and other help available such as housing

benefit and help for handicapped people.

NP.32 Your Retirement Pension
NP.32A Your Retirement Pension if You are Widowed or Divorced
NP.32B Retirement Benefits for Married Women
NI.92 Earning Extra Pension by Cancelling Your Retirement
NI.105 Retirement Pension and Widow's Benefit: payment direct into bank or building society accounts
NI.184 Non-contributory Retirement Pension for People over 80
NI.205 Attendance Allowance: cash help for disabled people who need a lot of attention or supervision
NI.211 Mobility Allowance: for people unable or virtually unable to walk
NI.229 Christmas Bonus: paid with some social security benefit
SB.1 Cash Help: you can claim supplementary benefit
SB.16 Supplementary Benefit: lump sum payments for special needs
SB.17 Help with Heating Costs for People Getting Supplementary Benefit
SB.18 Supplementary Benefit: the capital rule
SB.19 Supplementary Benefit: weekly payments for special needs
D.11 NHS Dental Treatment
G.11 NHS Glasses
H.11 Fares to Hospital
P.11 NHS Prescriptions
RR.1 Who Pays Less Rent and Rates?
HB.1 Help for Handicapped People
NI.9 Going into Hospital
NI.38 Social Security Abroad
NI.196 Social Security Benefit Rates and Earnings Rules
NI.248 New Ways of Claiming for Couples.

(Remember, too, that you can obtain information on benefits by ringing Freephone DHSS in some areas.)

This may seem a bewildering amount of information, and the confusion is compounded as there are plans for radical changes to the social security system to be phased in over the next twenty or so years, some measures to be implemented soon, others in the long term. So do not feel you have to struggle through the maze alone. If there are any points which seem to need clarification or any problems with your parent's retirement pension and benefit entitlement, it will be well worth your while, or better still for both of you, to make enquiries at your local social security office. The staff there, although often overworked, are very helpful and will be glad to sort out any problem you may have. (If possible, try to make an appointment.)

If a new idea recently tried out in two London health centres takes off, it may be easier to find out about elderly people's entitlements from a local health centre rather than from the DHSS office. A doctor at one of the large London teaching hospitals has devised a computer program which will calculate benefits on the spot; the program is the result of six years' work, carried out in co-operation with the DHSS. The doctor concerned notes that a third of those entitled to supplementary benefit do not claim it; GPs, he thinks, are in the ideal position to spot those who might be entitled to extra help and would benefit from it. So keep a look out locally in case your area is one of those with access to this valuable facility.

Likely sources of income for your parent will include the National Insurance retirement pension, supplementary pension and payments from the DHSS, pension from a previous employer's own superannuation scheme, pension from a private insurance scheme (especially if your parent was self-employed and contributed to a pension plan), investment income from savings, and any private grant from a charitable organization such as the British Legion.

Not only should you be looking at your parent's pension situation and other possible sources of financial help: there may be benefits to which you yourself are entitled, depending on individual circumstances. Obtain leaflet NI.212 from the DHSS, on invalid care allowance (ICA), a cash allowance for people under pensionable age who look after a disabled person. You do not have to be related to the disabled person or to live at the same address in order to claim. ICA counts as taxable income, but you need not have paid any national insurance contributions to get it. However, you may claim only one allowance even if you are looking after two people (e.g. both parents, or two aunts); you must be looking after a disabled person who gets either attendance allowance or constant attendance allowance with an industrial, war or service pension and you must spend at least 35 hours every week caring for him or her (with certain exceptions for holidays, for example, or if the disabled person is in hospital). An award of ICA entitles the carer to a Class I National Insurance credit for each week the allowance remains in payment. You must not be doing work for which you earn or expect to earn more than (at present) £12 a week, and there are various other requirements listed in the leaflet, which you will need to read carefully in the light of your own circumstances. If you are receiving certain benefits such as widow's or supplementary, these could invalidate your claim for ICA.

If you find it difficult to manage on the money you have coming in, you may be able to obtain supplementary benefit and help with your housing costs. You may also be entitled to free prescriptions, glasses, dental treatment and help with fares to hospital.

Another important point to consider if you are not able to work regularly because you stay at home to look after someone is that you will need to protect your basic retirement pension if you are not paying national insurance contributions. DHSS leaflet NP.27 (*Looking After Someone at Home? How to protect your pension*) will tell you about Home Responsibilities Protection (HRP) for your pension and when and how to apply.

A very useful booklet, *Help at Hand*, is produced by the Association of Carers and is, it says, 'a signpost guide for carers, covering benefits, services and the emotional aspect of caring'. See page 215 for details.

STATE BENEFITS FOR THE ELDERLY

This abridged list of benefits should only be regarded as a starting-point – firstly because space does not permit an exhaustive list of what is available, and secondly because you or your parent should check up at the time of retirement and at any other relevant time if you think there may be entitlements to claim, bearing in mind that regulations, payments and allowances change from time to time. The DHSS leaflet FB.2 *Which Benefit?* (available in Urdu, Gujerati, Hindi, Punjabi, Bengali and Chinese as well as English) will also be found useful.

Retirement pension This is for men over 65 and women over 60 who have retired from work (women will soon have the option to go on working to the same retirement age as men), but they do not have to have given up work completely. People who do not retire at the statutory age can earn extra pension. However, the current position is that pensions are paid regardless after 70 for men and after 65 for women, no matter how much work they do. Women who have paid their own contributions and widows (on their husband's contributions) receive the standard-rate basic pension. Wives or adult dependants and children receive an allowance on the husband's pension and married women not entitled to a pension on their own contributions may get an allowance on their husbands' contributions.

If a wife has made contributions other than at the reduced rate for married women, she may still not have made sufficient to give her the same amount that she would have received on her husband's contributions. In this case, the balance will be paid on the basis of her husband's contributions. It will be necessary, however, for her to enter the amount of her independent pension on an Income Tax Return because part of her earned income as a wife – which this pension will count as – is free of tax.

There are special rules for people who have been divorced or widowed and special provisions regarding earnings-related pensions, contracted-out schemes by firms and graduated pensions.

Over-80 pension This is for people aged 80 or over who are entitled to a NI retirement pension of (currently) less than £23 a week or none at all. To qualify, you must have lived in the UK for at least 10 years since you reached 60. Married women and widows whose husbands were born before July 1883 also qualify for a non-contributory pension. Ask at the local social security office.

Supplementary pension If a retired person cannot manage financially on his or her pension he or she may be able to get a supplementary pension in addition. The requirements are the same as for claiming supplementary benefit. It is paid to people who are not working full time and who do not have enough money to live on. It can be paid in addition to other benefits or earnings from part-time work, or if the person has no money at all. It cannot be claimed if the claimant has savings of more than £3000. If awarded, the recipient will also automatically get various health benefits and, if a tenant, help from the council with rent and rates, or, if an owner-occupier, help with rates. The health benefits will include free NHS glasses, dental treatment and hospital travelling (over retirement age, NHS prescriptions are automatically free). Lump-sum payments are also available, currently, for certain exceptional but essential one-off expenses. Leaflet SB.16, *Lump Sum Payments*, from local offices, contains further information.

Reduced fares Both men and women can buy British Rail Senior Citizens' Railcards if they are 60 or over. These last for a year and allow holders to buy some tickets at reduced prices. Some local transport services offer free or reduced-price travel on buses or on the London Underground. Enquire from British Rail Information Offices, London Regional Transport or your local bus service office.

Widows Most widows qualify for widow's allowance, except those of 60 or over whose husbands were receiving retirement pension when they died. The payment goes on for the first 26 weeks and after that there may be widowed mother's allowance or widow's pension. (It has been suggested that widows may instead of the allowance be given a lump-sum payment under new provisions to be implemented in the future.) Only the late husband's NI contributions count. Claim should be made on form BW1, obtainable from the local social security office.

The widow's pension is for women widowed at age 40 or over who have no dependent children or who are 40 or over when widowed mother's allowance ends. How much is paid depends on age when widowed and when widowed mother's allowance ends. If the husband died after 5 April 1979 his widow will get any earnings-related pension he has earned. This is usually paid automatically, but if it is not, get in touch with the local social security office.

Living abroad If planning to live abroad for a period and entitled to pensions, allowances, etc. your parents should ask for the DHSS leaflets NI.38 (*Social Security Abroad*) and SA.29 (*Your Social Security and Pension Rights in the EC*).

Going into hospital: effect on benefits and pensions If your parent has to go into hospital, some of his/her needs will be met by the NHS rather than by benefits and pensions, so while he/she is there, some of these may be reduced temporarily or stopped (check with the social security office or with leaflet N.19).

Disabled or handicapped people The possibility of getting help with rent and rates if pensions are inadequate has already been mentioned. There is also rate relief for disabled people and for those for whom special alterations or additions have had to be made to the home to help them cope with their disability. Either council or private tenants or owner-occupiers or a member of their household can apply. Obtain the leaflet RR.1 from council offices, library or a CAB, or from the social security office.

Attendance allowance makes provision for people aged two and over who need a lot of looking after because they are severely disabled, either mentally or physically. There are two rates, a lower one for either day or night attendance and a higher one to cover both day and night. It is an allowance worth applying for, as it may mean that a carer can still continue with his or her job if there is someone to 'cover' for her at home. The allowance is tax-free, non-contributory and non-means-tested. An award of attendance allowance does not normally affect entitlement to other benefits.

Mobility allowance is for disabled or handicapped people up to the age of 75, but they have to qualify before they are 65 and it must be claimed before they reach the age of 66. It is intended to help with the extra cost of getting around and it is paid every four weeks.

If your parent is disabled or handicapped he/she might benefit from the range of services provided by local authority services departments, depending on local circumstances and the local authority's assessment of his or her need. To cite some examples, the social services department may help with special aids for and adaptations to the home, home helps, day centres, meals-on-wheels, laundry, holidays, provision of television and telephone, and so on. DHSS leaflet HB.1, *Help for Handicapped People*, will give much useful advice not only on cash benefits but also on these other support services. If you live in Scotland, you will need *Help for Handicapped People in Scotland* from the Scottish Home and Health Department (see page 206).

The DHSS leaflet HB.2, *Aids for the Disabled*, may be obtained from the DHSS Leaflets Unit or from the DHSS Health Services Branch (see page 212 for both addresses). Also obtainable from the local social security office is the *Door to Door Guide* to transport for disabled people published by the Department of Transport; British Rail produces a leaflet entitled *The Railcard for Disabled People*, which is available from stations.

Injured in the forces Pensions may be paid to people who are disabled or bereaved as a result of service in the armed forces. A variety of leaflets is produced by the DHSS and your local social security office can put you and your parent in touch with the War Pensioners' Welfare Service for help and advice on war pension matters.

Lump-sum payments These may be made under the supplementary benefit scheme for a variety of exceptional but essential expenses which are not covered by the normal weekly supplementary benefit rates. No payment can be made unless all the conditions of the regulations are met in full. These conditions require, for example, that a person be entitled to a weekly payment of supplementary pension or allowance, or housing benefit supplement, on the day he or she makes the claim; has, generally speaking, not paid for the item or expense concerned before seeking help; does not have savings in excess of £500 out of which the expense could be met. Leaflet SB.16, *Lump Sum Payments*, which can be obtained from the local DHSS office, describes the items for which these payments can be made. Confidential advice about lump-sum payments may be obtained by contacting the DHSS Freephone service.

Otherwise it may be possible to get an 'exceptional needs' payment from a charity connected with the former profession or trade of the applicant or his widow. Check on the *Charities Digest*, which lists such bodies (see page 217). Alternatively, the elderly person's former employer (or employer of a deceased husband) might be willing to help, or such organizations as the British Legion or the unit in which a former serviceman served. The local Age Concern office can supply a list of local charitable organizations and their trustees.

GETTING THE BEST POSSIBLE INCOME

Apart from state pensions, your parent(s) may have other sources of income or have some capital to invest which can bring in extra money from such sources as building societies, 'granny bonds', national savings certificates, and so on. There are some good firms of financial advisers who will go through the person's financial affairs, come to an understanding of the kind of lifestyle he wants to enjoy and what his resources are to fulfil that desire, and advise on the best possible way of investing what he has to bring in an income, at the same time allowing for some capital growth as well to help keep pace with inflation. The best way of finding a good financial adviser is probably a recommendation from a friend who has already used his services, which are generally free. Otherwise the easiest and most readily available source of advice is probably the local bank manager, whose advice will certainly be sound, though he will not recommend the sort of investment – stock market speculation, for example – which has the potential to make (or lose) your parent a fortune.

Among the options to consider are the purchase of an annuity (that is, using a lump sum to provide an income for life for a husband and eventually his widow, or for either of them alone). This is, of course, a gamble as the annuity ends with the first or second life, but it has advantages in that the return on capital is usually higher than for any other form of investment and in that only part of the income is subject to tax. It is certainly necessary to shop around to get the best possible deal, and the elderly person must realize that once his capital is invested in an annuity, it cannot be left to his sons or daughters. The provision of an annuity can, of course, affect supplementary pension rights, and this should be borne in mind.

If your parent is really elderly, he or she may be able to take out a mortgage annuity on his or her home. This can be a capital sum up to 75 per cent of the value of the house, and could be invested to provide an income or used to buy an annuity. When the owner of the house dies, the loan is repaid from the sale of the house. Of course, it is possible to protect the interests of the surviving wife or husband with a survivorship annuity.

Bank deposit accounts can be another option. If the capital is to remain in the bank, it would be worth putting it in a high-interest account – with some banks it is possible to transfer money immediately if required to a current account. However, if your parent is not paying tax at the standard rate, he cannot reclaim tax paid by the building society or bank, so some other form of investment could be preferable.

National Savings Certificates are an excellent form of investment and are a government security. The money can be withdrawn at any time, together with any interest owing, but if they are kept in for a period of five years, the rate of interest is high and its value is not taxed. Enquire at your local post office for details.

'Granny bonds' or Index-linked Savings Certificates (now available to all) are another investment which is particularly sound in a time of high inflation. The investment is linked to the Retail Price Index, which proofs them against inflation; so if inflation is low you may lose out against some other investments, but if it is high you will win. The bonds can, of course, be cashed at any time, but if you do this within a year of purchase, only the purchase price is refunded; after one year but within five years, you get the purchase price plus an amount equal to the inflation for the period and an additional supplement (also index-linked). If the bonds are left in for the full five years, then the holder will receive an additional index-linked bonus. This may not seem a very high return on the face of it, but remember that the inflation-linked gain is free from income tax, investment surcharge and Capital Transfer Tax. More information is available from post offices.

Post Office Savings Bank accounts, either ordinary or investment, are another popular form of saving. The ordinary account allows for small deposits and the rate of interest is, currently, 3 per cent if the balance is under £500; 6 per cent if over £500; and the first £70 of interest is free of income tax (£140 for a married couple). Although interest rates fluctuate on the investment accounts, they are considerably higher than for the ordinary accounts and withdrawals can be made with one month's notice.

Premium Savings Bonds will appeal to those who like a bit of a gamble, but it is probably wise only to have a little 'flutter'. They are bought in groups of five at £1 each bond and become eligible to be included in the weekly draw when they have been owned for three months after the month in which they are bought. Every unit has the same chance of winning a prize. Bonds can be bought from any post office or bank, and if you have a win on them the winnings are free of income tax. They can be cashed at any time for the price paid for them.

It will probably be worth shopping around for the best banking deal if your parent has a current bank account, though he/she may wish to keep the account at a bank he has been used to dealing with and where he knows the manager.

INCOME TAX

Unfortunately, even after retirement age when one might hope for a respite from a lifetime of having to fill in returns, the income tax position still has to be watched, particularly if your parent has sources of investment income, annuities or the like. If there are any problems, or you and your parent find it difficult to sort out the form, it will be worth making an appointment with someone at the local Inland Revenue office and having a chat, as advised earlier. Staff will probably help with filling in the form, too, if your parent is having trouble.

The National Insurance retirement pension on its own will not make your parent liable to tax, nor will a state supplementary pension, but it may be that a graduated pension or additional pension for working on after retirement age may take him or her into the tax bracket. Remember that if you or other relatives make an allowance to your parent, this is not taxable.

Leaflet IR4, mentioned earlier, answers some of the questions pensioners ask, such as 'What must I pay tax on?'; 'What tax allowances can I claim?'; 'Do I pay tax on my widow's pension?'; 'How is the pension from my previous employer taxed?'; 'How do I pay tax on my NIRP?'; 'My wife has a pension of her own. What is the tax position?'; 'I am thinking of taking a part-time job. How will this affect my tax?'; 'I have saved some money and am thinking of buying an annuity. Will this annuity be taxed?'; 'I have some money invested in assurance policies. What is the tax position?'; 'I let part of the house I live in. Does this involve any income tax?' – and other common queries.

It is possible that your parent may be entitled to the special tax allowance for people over 65 whose incomes are less than a certain amount. Called 'age allowance', it is larger than the ordinary single or married allowance, which it replaces. It is not given automatically, so read leaflet IR4A, and if you think your parent may be entitled to it, advise him to get in touch with his tax office.

Other tax allowances may be claimable – for instance, dependent relative tax allowance, blind person's allowance or housekeeper allowance (further information is available from the local tax office).

Remember to advise your parent that if he or she writes to the tax office he should help it trace his papers by quoting the reference number from any previous correspondence. If he goes to the office, he should check that it will be open (hours of opening are not long – usually between 10 am and 4 pm, Monday to Friday) and take all his papers with him. When your parent knows he is going to get any pension, he should tell the tax office the starting date, the amount and where it comes from so that his code can be changed if necessary (otherwise he may later be faced with a bill for unpaid tax – this has often happened to pensioners who did not realize that their NIRPS pension, for instance, had to be taken into account when putting down all sources of income). If there are any changes in your parent's income or family circumstances which might affect his tax, he should let the tax office know as soon as possible.

LEGAL MATTERS

Legal matters can be complicated, so if in any doubt it is as well to consult a solicitor to get things sorted out to your parent's and your own satisfaction.

Most carers would be diffident about suggesting that their parents made a will, but in fact many old people feel easier in their minds to know that their affairs are settled and that any property or assets they are leaving will go to the people or organizations of their choice. Perhaps the right attitude is to get such matters sorted out satisfactorily and then put them out of one's mind.

A will form may be obtained from most stationers and, unless there are many complicated provisions, simply filled in, signed by the person making the will in the presence of two witnesses (present at the same time), who then sign the will themselves. It is usual to appoint two executors to see that the provisions of the will are carried out (if one of them is a solicitor, there is usually a clause stating that he can charge for work done in connection with administering the estate). Alternatively, your parent may feel happier if the will is drawn up professionally for him or her by a solicitor. A will may be changed or revoked at any time if the person making it so wishes. If a beneficiary under the will dies before the testator that legacy lapses and the property passes under any general gift in the will, unless a new bequest is added.

If your parent dies without making a will, there are certain set rules on inheritance and these should be checked with a solicitor, but first claim on the estate is for the funeral and administration of estate expenses, debts and any other liabilities.

A wide-reaching new law which has been widely welcomed, having come into force early in 1986, is the

'Enduring Power of Attorney'; this makes it far simpler and cheaper for relatives to manage the financial affairs and property for someone who becomes mentally incapable of looking after them. Up to the time of this Act, an elderly father, say, could grant his son, for example, power of attorney to manage his affairs, but if the father were to become incapacitated by mental illness the deed would lose its effectiveness – just when it was most needed. In such a case, the son would have to be appointed receiver by the Court of Protection (see page 213) so that, for instance, property could be sold and the proceeds used to provide nursing-home care for the parent.

Now, if an elderly parent appoints you his attorney under the new Act while he still has all his faculties, it will be possible for you to continue to act for him even if he can no longer remember who you are. However, the Enduring Power of Attorney deed should be drawn up while the parent still has all his faculties – if they have gone, it is too late for him to grant a power of attorney. If your parent so wishes, he can modify the power of attorney to take effect only if and when he can no longer cope.

The way it works is that your father (or mother) gives you a power of attorney. When you think he is becoming confused, forgetful or incapable you will have to give notice to him and to certain relatives (the categories are laid down) that you are going to register the power of attorney with the Court of Protection. If there are any objections, the Court will arbitrate. Once the power of attorney is registered, your parent will not be able to revoke it without the Court's agreement. Registration will allow you to carry out all the actions the deed allows; for example, unless the deed says otherwise, you will be able to sell your parent's property without her consent, if this is necessary to keep her, make small gifts to relatives on her behalf, and so on, and normally no accounts will have to be rendered (although they should be kept in case the Court wishes to check that funds have not been misused).

It is not necessary for a solicitor to draw up the document for you – forms are on sale at legal stationers, and a leaflet available from the Court of Protection explains how the scheme works in full detail. The only expense involved is a fee of £30 which is payable on registration. Considering that a startling one in ten of the over-65s suffer from senile dementia, the new law, with its built-in safeguards, should be very helpful in administering the affairs of elderly people adequately. It provides for them to choose and appoint someone they trust while they are still in possession of all their faculties, to look after their money and property for them at some future time should it become necessary.

If your parent has not been able to make an enduring power of attorney, or has chosen not to do so, and you need to manage his or her affairs, you can apply to the Court of Protection (at the address on page 213) to be appointed 'receiver'. You will need to get a doctor's certificate on a special form obtainable from the Court and you will have to give the Court full particulars of your parent's family and assets. Again, a leaflet is available from the Court dealing with the procedure. When you have been appointed receiver, you will be able to manage the financial affairs on your parent's behalf, under the Court's supervision. You will have to file an account every year and you may have to provide a security bond, but you will have the authority of the Court behind you to safeguard you and your parent. A fee of £50 is payable at the beginning, and an additional fee is payable every year on a sliding scale according to the income arising. But the Court has power to forgo or postpone fees in case of hardship. The Court is able (in appropriate cases) to make wills for people unable to do so themselves.

On legal matters generally, remember that CABs can help you find low-cost legal advice for you or your parent and advise whether Legal Aid would be available.

JULIE

For many years Julie helped to look after her husband Brian's old parents who lived in their own home nearby. It was a happy situation as they all got on well together, and Julie was able to take her mother-in-law into the nearest town to look at the shops and to keep an eye on both of them generally. When the couple were in their eighties, the old lady's health started to fail. She had a breast lump removed and later had a severe fall, breaking her leg and hip and having to undergo a hip replacement operation.

Her husband, although older than his wife, was more robust and was able to take over the cooking, washing and housework, but she felt her inactivity very much as she had always enjoyed preparing meals and running the house, and was still very lively in her mind. At the age of 85, her husband took up a new hobby – photography. He was a keen gardener and liked to take pictures of his plants with an instant camera. In fact, he would always try anything new and this flexible habit of mind seemed to keep him going and very young for his age, although like most elderly people he also enjoyed reminiscing about the 'old days'.

As they got older, Julie devised a system in case her in-laws had a sudden health problem or attack. She provided them with a fluorescent yellow card to put up in the window, and as soon as she or her husband got up in the morning they would look across to his parents' house to see if there was any need for them to go over there straight away.

One morning, the card was displayed: Julie's father-in-law had suffered his first heart attack. Her mother-in-law's condition deteriorated, and after a period of nursing at home and a spell in hospital, she eventually had to go into a private nursing home. While she was there, her husband had another attack, from which he died.

'The home was very expensive,' said Julie, 'and my mother-in-law was continually asking to come home. However, we felt we weren't qualified to nurse her, and we had had so little help from the medical and social services when she was at home that we thought she would be better off where she was with frequent visits from us. It certainly gave us a chance to observe at least this particular private home – she did not want to go into the long-stay local hospital, which still had, for her, as for many old people, the stigma of "workhouse".

'I must say that I agree with those people who say that some private homes must be run for the money – though of course there are obviously good ones. Every time we went, there were the six or seven old ladies just sitting in their chairs with nothing to occupy them. I vividly remember going one Saturday afternoon and finding them as usual in the sitting-room – with a rugby match on the TV! And no one came to change the channel for them – I suppose they were too diffident to do it for themselves.

'I'm sure more could be done to occupy them. So far as we could see, the staff just got them up and dressed in the morning and helped them to meals and to their chairs, took them to the lavatory if they rang the bell, and that was it.

'There was one old lady you could see was a bustling, busy, housewifely sort of body, who had, until she became infirm, looked after her brother at home. I'm sure she would love to have peeled vegetables and helped with any of the work in the home, given half a chance. All she could do was knit squares and she was bored stiff with it. Even the magazine she was given to look at by one of the staff was one she had seen before – it had probably been there for weeks.

'Another old lady had nothing to do except look through her handbag trying pathetically to find the key to her old house, which, of course, wasn't there. I actually heard one of the staff say to her, "Number 17 isn't your house any more, Mrs Marshall – someone else is living there now. Your room upstairs is where you live." So we realized that you can still be isolated and unoccupied, even in a home surrounded by other people. If only they had organized some card games, or bingo, or hired video films of nature programmes or something which would be fresh and interesting. As we live in the country, they don't get groups of volunteers going round as you do, I believe, in cities or large towns, helping to take the old people out or visiting them to chat or otherwise entertain them.

'Of course, my mother-in-law was too ill anyway to sit in the communal rooms, but we weren't over-impressed by the medical care either. Her feet and ankles swelled up while she was there – something which had not happened at home or in the hospital where she was treated. We could never find out what caused it and apparently, when the doctor did visit, he never looked at her feet, although we kept telling one or other of the staff that we thought he ought to know about it.

'We had no choice of home – they are very scarce in this area – but I suppose the lesson to learn is that you should look very carefully if you can choose where your parent goes, bearing in mind some of the points I have made.

'My only other advice on caring for elderly parents is to be

143

as patient as possible and find time to listen to them. They do love to talk about old times, and it really does make you think how hard some people lived fifty or sixty years ago, especially in country areas like ours.

'My mother-in-law died in the home after being there for about four months, and I still wonder if we should have had her back and tried to find a private nurse. But you can only do the best you can at the time, and we did feel she should have professional care.'

CHAPTER 9

Physical illnesses

A number of symptoms which appear in elderly people are put down simply to 'getting old', but in fact they may be signs of illness which can be treated, and treatment may well bring about their relief or disappearance – that is, if the symptoms appear gradually; should your parent's condition suddenly or markedly deteriorate, you should seek the doctor's advice at once.

It is sometimes difficult to admit that a parent can be seriously ill – in fact you cannot really believe that someone who looked after you from birth and always seemed able to help with your physical and emotional problems can be ill. When Jane's father had his first, minor, stroke she could not admit that it might presage a serious illness, particularly as her father's doctor made light of it too. His elderly neighbours, however, did not and warned her that it might be the beginning of a breakdown in his health. Jane was only convinced when he had a massive stroke a few weeks later, which led to his eventual death.

But it is very important to be sensitive to your parent's health and encourage him to have a thorough check-up if the symptoms of which he is complaining persist. It is easy to think that someone with a variety of ailments is suffering from hypochondria and ought to be able to 'snap out of it', but the odds are that the symptoms are quite genuine and need treatment.

Very often a change in personality, irritability and rejection can signal illness, although the visiting relatives may see only difficult behaviour or hurtful rudeness. Such signs should always be interpreted as a cry for help, particularly if they are uncharacteristic of the person concerned. Alternatively, the elderly person may become very gentle and withdrawn – again, if this is uncharacteristic, it could be a bad sign.

Illness frequently takes a different course in old people from what it does in young ones. Cancer, for instance, may be only slowly progressive in the elderly, and the old person may die of some quite different illness, whereas a young person in her thirties could succumb in a matter of months. Bad colds or 'flu can be much more serious in the old than in the young and sometimes illnesses are 'submerged', that is, show very few open symptoms apart from general lassitude and feeling unwell. If your parent is normally active but suddenly has no energy and wants to stay in bed for several days, it may be indicative of infection or a warning that a heart attack is in the offing. It is far better to seek medical advice if there is any doubt at all, rather than dismissing the symptoms or change in behaviour as being simply a little 'turn' or upset.

Many elderly people become obsessed with their own health or ailments, although they may not have been so when they were younger. Whatever the topic under discussion, they always seem to manage to bring it back to illness, sometimes other people's but more particularly their own. In bad cases their complaints may be continuous, in spite of regular visits from the doctor and specialist check-ups which have failed to reveal anything serious. It is very difficult to sort out complaints about genuine aches and pains and decide how serious they are. Your parent may truly feel discomforts of various kinds, which anxiety has magnified into much worse symptoms. Or she may in fact be suffering from something which has not been revealed by a medical check-up. One has to give the elderly person the benefit of the doubt, hard as it may be to live with, and keep in touch with her GP. It may be necessary, too, to keep a watchful eye on her medicine cabinet – you may find it is overloaded with over-the-counter remedies and that she is taking far too many unprescribed pills and potions.

The following are some illnesses which may come in old age, which will give an indication of possible symptoms to look out for. Do not jump to conclusions at the least little variation from the norm, however, or fear the worst if your mother exhibits a little slowness in going upstairs or has a slight cough sometimes. Always, if in doubt, consult the doctor.

STROKES

When Deirdre had a stroke, she was alone in the house. Her husband was out and their children, grown up and married, lived some distance away. She was found by a neighbour, unconscious on the floor of her bedroom. The stroke, or cerebral haemorrhage, had paralysed her down the right side, and had completely deprived her of the ability to speak. Deirdre was admitted to hospital in a serious condition, although she soon recovered consciousness. The stroke, as so often happens, had come completely without warning, although for her age and height Deirdre was grossly overweight. In other cases, a minor stroke, causing only weakness, slightly impaired vision and other small symptoms, can be a prelude to something more severe.

The fact that Deirdre recovered consciousness quite quickly was a good sign, and in spite of the fact that at first she was incontinent, could not move or stand up, had badly impaired vision and was unable to speak, she eventually made a good recovery. She was an intelligent and highly motivated woman and she was determined to use every available bit of help and 'coaching' to recover as much as possible of her lost faculties. After weeks of hard work and devoted help from her husband, family, friends and the specially trained nursing and auxiliary staff at the hospital, she was able to go home, speak again (if not quite normally) and eventually get upstairs and take an active part in running the house. Although her arm and hand were still partly paralysed, she could work on a tapestry, one of her hobbies before she was taken ill.

One of the worst things she had to contend with was depression, and this is characteristic in stroke victims. It may sometimes seem that recovery is painfully slow, not inch by inch but millimetre by millimetre. It requires every ounce of the patient's energy and determination and plenty of optimism and encouragement from her family to pull her back towards normal life.

It is very important, if you are visiting a parent who has had a stroke, to try your best to communicate with her, even if she shows no signs of responding. Sometimes a patient can hear what you are saying and understand it, although she may not be able to make a reply. And a

147

demonstration of affection, such as a kiss or holding a hand, may well get through to her, even though the hand you are holding may seem inert and devoid of life.

It is often uncertain at the beginning how things will end. With Jane's father, for instance, his last stroke was progressive and he died within ten days. Deirdre, however, had made good progress towards recovery after only two months. One of her main worries was that she would be a continuous burden to her husband, who was considerably older than she was and not strong, and this contributed to her feelings of uselessness and depression. Later on, she knew he needed a holiday and wanted him to go away and have a complete rest and change, taking up his hobby of looking for antiquarian books, but she could not repress her tears and feelings that she was a nuisance and in the way. However, her eldest daughter offered to spend her annual holiday looking after her, so her husband was able to have a break with an easy mind and Deirdre had the motivation of giving her daughter a good time and as much of a holiday as possible in her country cottage.

If your parent makes a good recovery in hospital and is likely to be able to return home, it will be necessary to sort out how she will be cared for there and what needs to be done to ensure that she will be able to continue to improve. This will take hard work, planning and application, so allow as much time as possible for it. It may be that if your parent was living alone she may have to stay with you or another member of the family for a while, or you may need to have a radical re-think about her future (although this, perhaps, can be put off for a while until she is established outside hospital). First talk to the hospital staff – doctor, sister, therapists of various kinds – and the social worker, so that you know what changes will be needed in the house where she will be staying and what local health workers will need to visit in order to continue her treatment and therapy. It will probably be necessary for you, or whoever will be caring for her, to find out and understand any remedial exercises she should be doing and what occupations will best help her regain the use of her manual skills, as in some areas it may not be possible for many home visits to be made by trained staff. If friends and family drop in as often as possible it will help to keep your parent interested and alert and combat the depression inherent in her illness. Plenty of praise for what has been achieved and patient sympathy for her disability will be a great help at this time.

Once basic skills, even simple ones which we all take for granted, such as dressing, eating without help, going to the lavatory, have become easier – thanks to patient help and perhaps a few simple aids and easy-to-manage clothing – your parent will feel far more independent. It may be, however, that the stroke caused such severe damage that not much progress is possible. Take the advice of the doctor, and do not push your parent into trying to attempt more than she is physically or mentally capable of managing. Any incentive you can give for trying to recover will be positive and helpful, but it is no good trying to 'jolly along' someone who is really not capable of responding.

HEART PROBLEMS

The symptoms of heart disease may be very obvious or quite the reverse. If we have no experience of it, we may think that it is characterized by bad chest or arm pains, blueness of the face, rapid pulse rate and difficulty in breathing, together with collapse. However, there are many other signs (which may however apply to other illnesses) to keep an eye open for. If the ankles are very swollen, or your parent has headaches, indigestion, a feeling of sickness, coughing fits, tiredness and lassitude, inability to sleep, they may all be signs that good circulation is not being maintained, and that therefore some of the organs of the body are not functioning with their usual efficiency.

It is always a good idea for an elderly person to have a regular medical check-up, say once a year, as a matter of routine; if this is established, it should not cause your parent to worry unduly. Heart disease may be a major killer, but if heart problems are diagnosed and treated, and your parent leads a well-regulated life, the chances of controlling it are good. She should watch her weight, if she has a tendency to overweight, take gentle exercise as

much as possible and keep calm, avoiding stress whenever she can. It is advisable to cut down on alcoholic
drinks, strong coffee and tea, dairy produce and eggs.
Smoking should be completely 'out' – though this may be
easier said than done.

A coronary attack is characterized by very bad chest
pains, paleness, sweating, a feeling of overwhelming
foreboding and eventual collapse. The patient should be
made comfortable, lightly covered and given plenty of air
and the doctor called immediately. Usually the patient
will be taken to hospital and treated in an intensive care
unit, then kept in for a further period of time until well
enough to return home.

One very common form of heart disease is angina,
which produces, usually after exertion, sudden severe
pains in the chest and arm (generally the left arm). There
are tablets which can relieve this pain very quickly once
they are placed under the tongue, but of course an attack
of angina can be so severe as to cause damage to the heart
or even death.

It is very natural to feel alarmed and worried if you have
suffered a heart attack, and to live in continual
apprehension of another one, which might well prove
fatal. As a carer, try to be as reassuring as possible, and
encourage your parent to live a normal life as far as he or
she can, with as many social distractions as are available.
She may try to exert herself and do too much, feeling that
time is running out, but this is just as much to be gently
discouraged as the attitude that she dare not do anything
for fear of another attack. If you can quietly keep her 'on
line' with her regime of sensible eating, exercise and
cutting down on alcohol and cigarettes, you will be doing
her the greatest possible service, for it is only too easy,
when one feels better, to neglect the very precautions
which are going to keep one that way.

Interest in life is very important – to everyone, of
course, but particularly to someone who has had a major
and frightening illness. Encourage your parent to take up
whatever she was doing before she was ill, if the doctor
says she is well enough. Particularly if she was working or
doing voluntary service of some kind, it will be good for
her spirits if she can go back again, perhaps putting in

fewer hours at first, unless the degree of responsibility she was shouldering would be too stressful.

COUGHS AND LUNG PROBLEMS

You should suspect your parent of having bronchitis if he has a cough which will not get better, produces a lot of phlegm, and has attacks of wheezing and breathlessness. If he also smokes or is overweight, these could be contributory factors. Medical treatment should be sought or the condition could get worse, and it can be treated with appropriate drugs. It is best if your parent can avoid contact with people with heavy colds or 'flu. If he has a very bad bronchial attack, get medical help immediately.

Emphysema, in which the small air cells of the lungs are partly obstructed, causing the circulatory system and the heart to be affected, can follow on from bronchitis. It is characterized by breathlessness. Ongoing treatment is essential and again it is very necessary to protect your parent from contact with other people's colds.

Lobar pneumonia, in which the whole of the lobe of the lung is affected by inflammation, is a result of infection by bacteria or viruses. It comes on suddenly with pain in the side, rapid breathing, a high temperature and persistent cough. It used to take a high toll in the days before antibiotics, particularly among the elderly, but it can now be controlled by the right treatment combined with careful nursing. In bronchopneumonia there are small patches of inflammation throughout the lungs, with accompanying discomfort in breathing and probably pains in both sides of the chest. As well as treatments with antibiotics, the sick room should be kept moist with a steam kettle and heart stimulants may be needed. It is essential to have skilled nursing, and your parent may have to be admitted to hospital for a while until she recovers.

EYE PROBLEMS

Glaucoma is very often 'picked up' these days by an optician during a routine eye test for new spectacles. Henry, for example, discovered that he had the condition in just this way when he was 63. His vision was very good for his age and he had absolutely no symptoms, although if the glaucoma had not been diagnosed and treated it could have led eventually to pain in the eyes, disturbed vision and even blindness. The condition is caused by increase in pressure from the fluid in the eyeball which is not being dispersed efficiently and which can eventually damage the optic nerve. If action is taken in time, it is possible to correct this pressure with courses of eyedrops which may have to be used for a long time, possibly for the rest of the patient's life. Alternatively, surgery can often cure the condition completely.

Cataract is a condition in which the lens of the eye turns opaque so that the patient can no longer see to read or write. It is now possible to replace the lens, in what is usually a very successful operation. Alternatively, the lens is removed and the patient wears special spectacles.

Sudden loss of clear vision or impaired sight can be a sign of a minor stroke, as Jane found with her father. So do report any problem of this nature, or any eye pains, to the doctor immediately.

If your parent should become partially sighted or completely blind, there are very many aids and amenities available, ranging from the provision of 'talking books' to the adaptation of the home, and the possibilities should be completely explored both with your local social services department and with such organizations as the Royal National Institute for the Blind. If your parent loses her sight late in life it will probably seem the most awful blow that fate could have dealt her, and she may, quite understandably, appear inconsolable. Unobtrusive practical help will mean a lot at this time, and any way you can encourage her to continue with her previous interests and friends will be the best possible boost for her morale. It is better not to try to minimize the extent of her loss, but to show that you understand what she is feeling and sympathize fully with her.

COLD-RELATED PROBLEMS
The severe February of 1986 again highlighted the plight of many old people who cannot afford to keep themselves and their homes warm enough during the bitter winter weather. It has been calculated that for every degree by which the average winter temperature drops, there is an

increase in mortality in the winter months of about 8,000, and many of these deaths occur among the elderly. As a leader in *The Times* said: 'For an unknown number of the elderly, there is nothing inevitable about death. It is as chancy as a coin for the gas meter slot, the confidence that they can afford a few hours of electric fire. Hypothermia is a cruel death and death by cold in penury is hard for a civilized society to bear without questioning its own worth.'

Another item in the press reported: 'An inquest will be held into the death from hypothermia and a heart attack of a widow, Mrs Ellen Robinson, aged 79, at a complex of old people's bungalows in High Wycombe, Buckinghamshire, where she was found collapsed beside her living-room fire. The warden, Ms Elma Camley, said, "She was too frightened to warm her place in case she could not pay the bills. I have pleaded with the DHSS to help my old people pay their bills, but they often refuse – and that's a death sentence." '

It is to be hoped that the urgent representations made after the terrible hardships suffered by many old people will now have some effect and that action will be taken at government level to see that people in need are helped and helped adequately. It is not enough that organizations such as Age Concern were in February 1986 distributing as a matter of urgency cold-weather survival kits worth about £20 each, containing thermal underwear, fuel stamps, a powdered drink, chocolate, soup, advice on keeping warm and on allowances which old people may be able to claim. They should not have had to be doing it. We should all be putting on pressure so that it will not again be necessary.

But what, after all, *is* 'hypothermia'? When we are young, our bodily mechanism which adjusts to ambient temperatures and compensates for cold and heat works efficiently. In elderly people the mechanism tends to work less well and certain illnesses – and even some prescribed drugs – can also have a further damaging effect.

This is why it is so important that old people should be warmly dressed in cold weather and have adequate bedding and heating. If your parent is living alone, you must be sure that she will keep herself warm enough, and if not, you should take measures to see that she does. Her ability to know when she is cold may be impaired, so she may not take the appropriate action to keep warm, even if she has the means to do so, and she may well sit reading, feeling all right but gradually getting colder and colder (see Fran's story, page 122).

How do you recognize a case of hypothermia if you are unlucky enough to encounter it? The patient may appear pale and feel very cold in the body (feel the abdomen, which should, in normal circumstances, always be warm); her breathing, too, may be laboured and slow. On the other hand, she may appear flushed and may not be aware of feeling cold. She may appear confused and forgetful. Call medical help at once and meanwhile wrap her warmly and turn up all available heat in the room. Do not try to raise her temperature too quickly by putting her into a hot bath or packing her round with hot water bottles – it could kill her.

Make sure that there is a room thermometer somewhere in the house if your parent is living on her own. A temperature of 65°F/18°C is advisable; a sitting-room should ideally be at 70°C/21°C.

Check with the social services to see what help towards paying fuel bills would be available in your parent's area; this may vary from district to district, but it is well worth finding out.

As we have seen, many elderly people are afraid of using their heating in case they cannot meet the bill when it comes and are then 'cut off'. An elderly friend living on a retirement estate in a town on the south coast of England recently wrote that while he was warm (but he dared not think about the cost), if he looked out of his window at other houses, he knew that none of his elderly neighbours had their central heating turned on, although the temperature was well below freezing outside. There are various ways in which you can help your parent to feel more secure on this score and prepare ahead for a winter fuel bill. First of all, make sure that the house is on the most economical tariff for heating and water heating. With electricity, for instance, a system of time switches combined with Economy 7 and night storage heaters could provide much cheaper heating and hot water than using an immersion heater and fan heaters during the day, providing the initial cost of the installation could be covered. The local electricity and gas showrooms and the Solid Fuel Advisory Service would give useful advice if you and your parent were thinking of changing the heating system in her house or wish to get the most economical service from the existing system.

To even out the cost, there are various measures your parent can take. The fuel industries have a scheme, for example, for spreading out the cost over a year, in twelve monthly payments. One can buy savings stamps or make weekly cash payments, or ask at the local coal merchant if this system of payment would be possible for solid fuel. It is sometimes advantageous to have a 50p-in-the-slot electricity meter installed, so this too could be considered. Your parent might like to open a special Post Office savings account making regular weekly payments, the money to be used when a fuel bill drops through the letter-box. Look out for a leaflet called *Electricity and Gas Bills for Your Home – how to pay them, how to get help if there is real hardship*, available from gas and electricity showrooms.

If your parent is considering changing her heating system, perhaps because it has become too much to carry coal for fires, there is a good booklet available from your local CAB called *Compare Your Home Heating Costs*. The following list shows which type of heating is the most efficient – that is, which supplies the most heat per £1 of money spent on it. Of course it is not exact, as the assessment is naturally affected by the efficiency with which the user manipulates the system

Most economical Closed anthracite stoves, gas convector heaters
Moderately economical (1) Electric storage heaters, new solid-fuel fires, gas radiant/convector fires
Moderately economical (2) Old solid-fuel fires, paraffin heaters, gas radiant fires
Least economical Electric fires, bottled propane and butane gas.

Enquire about the following at the local electricity board's showrooms or offices: easy-payment schemes; appliances; choosing the best tariff; operating and setting controls on heating appliances, etc. (a home visit can be arranged); aids for the disabled; insulation.

Gas showrooms and offices have similar facilities on offer, plus free safety checks for old people living on their own.

An insulated house is a snug house – but remember that you should not seal up every ventilation gap, which could be dangerous where paraffin, solid-fuel or bottled gas appliances are used because they consume oxygen during the combustion process. (From time to time people have suffocated in caravans because they have closed up all the cracks and gone to sleep while a heating appliance is in use.)

However, it might be worth considering blocking off the fireplace in the main living-room if it is not being used (a painted sheet of hardboard would be suitable, with small holes drilled at intervals for ventilation). Consider, too, sealing doors and windows with draught-excluder strip. Check the floor and insulate any gaps with layers of newspaper or carpet underlay. Line the curtains (milium interlining, which reflects heat back into the room, is a good buy) or make curtains of some heavy fabric. Hang a curtain over the living-room door. Use double glazing on the window – either a sheet of glass held in place with turning flanges or, even cheaper, clear plastic food wrap stretched and tacked on to a simple wooden frame.

The loft should be insulated in all houses, using at least 4 inches of insulating material such as glass-fibre wool or vermiculite chips. It is worth enquiring whether any financial aid would be available for this. Some councils, for example, will pay for the cost of the materials, though not for installation – a dirty but by no means difficult job. If you or your parent cannot carry out this work, try Age Concern for volunteers. Owner-occupiers can apply for an improvement grant from their local authority towards the cost of insulating lofts, tanks and pipes.

Thermal underwear is a good idea for elderly people, and there are various warm housecoats or quilted 'bags' for use indoors in cold weather. A duvet on the bed is both warm and light: choose one with the warmest 'tog' rating (ask the assistant's advice when buying it). Exercise every day helps to maintain good circulation if your parent can manage it, although in snowy or icy weather she will probably not want to venture out much in case of falling.

Remember that food plays an important part in keeping old people warm. A bowl of hot soup is an instant warmer and can be left in a vacuum flask if necessary for your parent to open and eat for lunch. There are plenty of thick varieties available in cans which are more of a meal than simply a starter; wide-necked vacuum flasks can be used in the same way, filled with a portion of stew and vegetables or similar meal for lunch.

When you have done all you can towards helping your parent to get herself a warm house – with warmth she can pay for – you must then leave it to her. Some elderly people do not like a house that feels too warm to them – particularly a warm bedroom – and if they have been used to solid-fuel appliances or open fires, they may distrust gas or electric heating and even, psychologically, find it not so warm. If you cannot get your parent to turn the heating on when it is clearly needed, despite all your urging, your only recourse is to her doctor, a social worker or a visiting nurse, if there is one. Often advice from the family may be disregarded, whereas the voice of authority carries more weight! Ultimately, however, having done all you can, you will have to let your parent, if she is capable of it, make her own decisions and lead her own life so far as her house is concerned.

HEARING PROBLEMS
It is quite usual for people to begin to hear less well as they grow older, but for most it is not a severe problem. Perhaps your parent finds she needs to have the television sound turned up, even though you can hear it perfectly well, or she cannot hear when the telephone rings. It may be difficult to get your parent to admit that she is unable to hear as well as she used to, as she may be afraid of people shouting at her all the time to make sure she can hear them, or worry that people will not bother to include her in conversation. However, if you can get her to talk about it, try to persuade her to have a word with her doctor. The source of the problem may simply be wax

in the ears and this can easily be removed from time to time.

If the problem is more serious, the doctor may refer her to a specialist, who may suggest surgery or more probably a hearing aid. These are now very unobtrusive and can transform life for a partly deaf person. Perhaps your parent would agree to attend classes in lip reading, which would enable her to tell you how you can best help her to understand what you are saying. This will probably involve you sitting where the light falls on your face and speaking fairly slowly – though not necessarily loudly. Perhaps her hearing is better in one ear than the other: if this should be the case, check which side she would prefer you to sit.

Some hearing aids are obtainable under the NHS, but NHS aids are not suitable for every kind of deafness so it may be necessary to obtain one privately. If so, it would be a good idea for you or a friend with good hearing to go along with your parent to the supplier; also, a trial period with the aid should be arranged before the decision to buy is taken.

Some people experience difficulties when first using a hearing aid, and this is why it is so necessary to try one out in case the problems persist. Hearing aids are expensive, too, so do make sure your parent first receives medical advice, and do check whether an NHS aid might be suitable before spending money on a commercial one. Apart from the initial cost, servicing and batteries will have to be paid for, whereas NHS aids are serviced and batteries provided free.

If your parent is only slightly hard of hearing, there are devices which can help. Telephone bells can be made to sound louder and there are some which flash a light as well as ring. Adaptations can be made to televisions and radios, too.

Write to the Royal National Institute for the Deaf (see Chapter 12) for useful leaflets for both hard-of-hearing and profoundly deaf people. You may find in your area a social worker who specializes in advice for the deaf. If so, she will be able to offer advice and to link your parent with people and organizations who can help her in practical matters and provide social contacts as well.

CONSTIPATION

This is a problem which worries old people considerably – probably a residual worry from their own childhood when, if they did not have a bowel movement each day, they were probably dosed with such laxatives as syrup of figs or Beecham's Pills or castor oil. Many elderly people have been in the habit of taking a daily laxative for many years, so that their bowels have lost the ability to function normally, but it is now taken for granted that the right kind of diet is far better than medicine, which should be reserved for when it is really needed. In fact, there is no law which says that a person should have a bowel movement once a day – it is entirely individual and depends on many factors, one of which obviously is how much food a person is eating. Many old people take less exercise than previously and eat less food, and therefore do not need to pass a motion so often as they have less bulk to get rid of.

If your parent worries about being constipated, it is a good idea to get him to see his doctor so that he can be reassured that he is not seriously ill (in any case, if constipation suddenly occurs for no obvious reason, such as change of diet or illness, a doctor should be consulted). It may be that some drug he is taking is causing it, or he could be suffering from depression, which can also account for it.

His diet may contain too much carbohydrate-rich food such as cakes and pastries made with white flour and not enough bulk of fibre for the bowel to work on, as provided by whole-grain cereals (contained in porridge, breakfast cereals such as All-Bran, and wholemeal bread), vegetables and fruit. With too little bulk, the bowel functions more slowly, resulting not only in constipation but sometimes also in diverticulitis. In this illness, the increased pressure in the abdomen, caused by lack of bulk, causes the bowel lining to 'bulge' through the muscular wall of the bowel in various parts, forming little pockets in which undigested food lodges, an ideal breeding ground for bacteria.

As observed earlier, it is not always easy to get older people to change over to eating wholemeal bread, 'roughage' and more vegetables if they have always been used to white bread and confectionery made with white flour, so it may be better to concentrate on trying to persuade them to mix a few spoonfuls of All-Bran with their usual breakfast cereal and getting them to eat an extra helping of vegetables (sweet corn is particularly good). Do not make light of your parent's worries in this direction – they are worries which many old people share. Show him or her that you take the problem seriously and would like to help solve it as far as possible.

PILES

This very uncomfortable complaint, common in old age, is one which many people are very embarrassed to mention. Its medical name is haemorrhoids, and you may find that using this term enables your parent to discuss it more freely – it sounds more official. The problem is also often suffered by pregnant women, so if you had piles when expecting a baby it may also help your parent if you can tell him or her that you too have experienced them and know how painful they can be.

Piles are a form of varicose vein which are found round the anus. Sitting down a lot can cause them to develop and constipation makes them worse. In fact, it is a vicious circle, as the pain of passing a motion makes the sufferer try to delay doing so, which causes even harder and more painful motions when they do occur. Piles often bleed and itch, and make sitting down very uncomfortable indeed.

Sufferers should consult their doctor if they have piles and see what he recommends. It is essential to keep the anal area very clean and dry and to use cream or lotion only on medical advice. Piles were often removed surgically in the past, but only if there is a great deal of blood loss is this now recommended.

OBESITY

Overweight in old people can contribute to many disorders and make them more severe, and can also be the cause of slower recovery from illness than would take place in a slimmer person. It is, of course, often very difficult for an older person to lose weight. She may not be able to take the exercise she once did, and too strict a diet may make her miserable and take away much of her remaining pleasure in life. However, diabetes, chest complaints, arthritis and foot problems are just a few of the conditions made worse by being obese, so it would be a good idea to check with your parent's doctor if he thinks that some effort at losing weight would be a good idea. It may be that drugs are being prescribed which make it very difficult for the consumer to stay slim, however, and certain illnesses are known to cause sufferers to gain weight.

As with anyone at any age, incentives are needed to get slim. If your parent has a good feeling about herself and still wants to look attractive and well dressed, that is half the battle. If she can still attract compliments from her friends on looking good, she will be more likely to keep to a modified diet and perhaps join a Weight Watchers' club, or other local slimming organization.

Encourage her (or him) to take more exercise. In the case of younger people, commuting, working, rushing about doing the shopping in the lunch hour, fitting in a host of activities in the day during one's working life all contribute to keeping the weight down – so does worry about work! In its place should be some other regular exercise. Many elderly people take up bowls or golf. Yoga is good for people of any age and although it is mainly women who go to yoga classes, they would benefit men equally. Swimming and walking are also good. But it is worth remembering that if the exercise your parent fancies looks like being at all strenuous, she should get her doctor's permission first.

BROKEN BONES
As people grow older, their bones become more brittle, and a fall which, in a younger person, might not be particularly serious can easily cause a fracture. If your parent has a fall and breaks a bone, call for a doctor or an ambulance immediately but do not try to treat the fracture yourself. The patient will probably be suffering from shock, so cover her with a warm rug or blanket and tuck a hot water bottle in with her. Do not attempt to move her, and do not give her anything to drink in case she has to be given an anaesthetic. Try to reassure her as much as possible and make sure that you, or someone else she

knows, goes with her if she has to go to hospital, so that you can let the staff know of her home circumstances and provide any other details that may be necessary.

LEGS AND FEET
Problems with legs and feet are very common in the elderly, and it is worth taking precautions early on to avoid some of the more usual ones. Varicose veins often occur, causing some people very little trouble and others a good deal of pain, nagging like an aching tooth. In the latter case, they should be treated by the doctor; otherwise, to stop them becoming a problem it will help if your parent is not overweight and takes exercise in the way of regular gentle walks to improve her circulation. If the veins are very bad, the skin may ulcerate or bleed, and this certainly calls for medical attention.

Foot problems can also be caused by bad circulation, but rheumatism, diabetes and lack of proper support for the feet can also cause pain and difficulty in walking. Properly fitted shoes, which give support to the feet, are a good long-term investment for foot health. There should always be a gap of half an inch between the end of the toes and the ends of the shoes, and the shoes must be wide enough for comfort. Check that shoes are a good fit by standing in stockinged feet on a piece of card and drawing round the feet, then cutting out the shapes and trying them in the shoes. If the card is too big or too small, the shoes are not the correct size. Your parent should always buy shoes in the afternoon, as feet swell during the day, and she should wear new shoes for short periods at a time during the first week. Feet should always be dry before shoes and socks or stockings are put on, and if shoes get wet they must be thoroughly dried before being worn again. If there are problems with the feet, first check with the doctor, as these may be a symptom of some other illness rather than a case for the chiropodist. He should be able to advise. See the leaflet *Fitter Feet* produced by Help the Aged and sponsored by Mycota (see Chapter 12).

WOMEN'S DISORDERS
Various problems associated with the organs of reproduction can surface in old age. A prolapse, for example,

whereby the uterus drops down into the vagina, can cause backache, incontinence and a feeling of 'pulling down' in the lower part of the abdomen. An operation is usually very successful – Jane's mother said she felt 'like a new woman' after she had surgery for her prolapsed womb. Other treatment can be given by a physiotherapist or by the insertion of a ring. Exercise to strengthen the pelvic muscles could help, too.

Fibroids or cysts can sometimes cause the need for a hysterectomy (removal of the womb, ovaries and fallopian tubes) even though there is no malignancy or if there is a pre-malignant condition. It may be necessary to reassure your mother about the operation, which is nowadays not nearly such a serious matter as it was some years ago. The techniques are much more advanced, and though there may be a few days of discomfort, recovery is usually very quick. However, rest is necessary at home when the patient leaves hospital.

Cystitis, or infection of the bladder, is more common in women (it can occur at any age) although men can also have it. It is a most uncomfortable and depressing illness, causing the sufferer to feel that she constantly wants to pass water, even if she has just been to the lavatory, and when she does go there is a burning sensation which can be very painful. The lower part of the abdomen aches and the urine may contain blood. Very often the temperature rises and the patient feels very much under the weather. It is essential to get treatment; until the doctor comes, encourage your parent to drink as much water or barley water as she can take. He will prescribe a course of medication, the whole course of which must be finished to clear up the infection. Ask if there are any instructions to be observed while taking the medication – certain tablets prescribed for cystitis, for instance, carry the warning that the patient should not be exposed to sunlight while taking them. Apart from the fact that it is very uncomfortable and unpleasant, an attack of cystitis should not be neglected as it can sometimes affect the kidneys. If there are frequent attacks, further investigation may be necessary.

While it is not certain what causes cystitis, one obvious precaution is to keep the genital area very clean to make sure that no infection is carried from the faeces into the urethra, whence it can travel to the bladder. If a daily bath or shower is not possible, a thorough washing of this area with pieces of cotton wool, to be disposed of after use, is advisable, particularly after passing a motion. Make sure that the area is well dried afterwards.

PROSTATE TROUBLE

One of the most common problems which can affect your father is enlargement of the prostate gland, and this usually manifests itself in increased 'frequency' or desire to pass water, without the ability to do so. Alternatively, there may be sudden incontinence. In all such cases, medical attention should be sought at once. Any increase in frequency calls for an examination by the doctor, as it may be necessary to operate on the prostate gland. Reassure your parent that this does not necessarily mean that there is malignancy present and that treatment or an operation usually gives permanent relief.

INCONTINENCE

Losing control of the bladder or bowels or both is something that most old people dread more than any other single physical affliction of old age. The same goes for their carers, too. So much emphasis was laid on early potty-training when our parents were young that the idea of not, so to speak, being 'trained' themselves can lead to great humiliation and depression. Perhaps the more relaxed attitude of younger generations towards potty-training may eventually lead to a more relaxed acceptance of incontinence in old age and a more matter-of-fact attitude towards dealing with it.

There are many causes of incontinence, one of the most usual being brain disorders such as dementia or acute confusion. A stroke can also result in loss of control of the muscles which open and close the urethra or, when the patient is partially mobile again, he may not be able to get to the lavatory in time or undress himself quickly enough. Any other condition which results in decreased mobility, such as painful feet or rheumatic joints, for example, can also delay the elderly person in getting to a commode or lavatory.

Sometimes prescribed drugs can result in incontinence – for instance, if your parent is taking strong sedatives, she may not be aware of the need to empty her bladder; diuretics, which combat water-retention, can result in an urgent need to pass water which may not be answered in time. Infections of the urinary tract, or prostate problems, are further causes, and so is a prolapse, which may result in stress incontinence, when a dribble of urine is expelled if the sufferer laughs, coughs or sneezes unexpectedly. Constipation can also bring about urinary incontinence.

If your parent is living in her own home, she may try her best to deal with her problem herself and even to conceal the fact that there is one. She will try to cope with extra washing and may well stop going out unless it is absolutely necessary in case she has an accident. Anxiety can make the condition worse, as we all know. Who hasn't felt the need to rush to the lavatory before going into an examination room or when waiting for a job interview? It is very necessary to look for the signs and persuade her to go to the doctor for a thorough check-up. The underlying cause may need specialist help to diagnose, but it may well be that there is treatment which can alleviate this distressing condition.

If not, it may be possible to provide some practical help. For instance, if mobility is the problem, take a good look at the house. As suggested earlier, it might be helpful to have a commode in an accessible place, a rail or frame or raised toilet seat to help the old person use the lavatory. Also advisable is clothing which is quick and easy to unfasten.

Physiotherapy to deal with stress incontinence and treat stroke sufferers so that they are able to get about better may also be a possibility. It is a good idea if your parent can get into the habit of using the lavatory regularly, say every two hours, and she should not restrict the amount of fluid she drinks as this can cause other problems. However, she should drink more in the morning when she is up and about than in the evening before going to bed, while not taking less liquid over all.

Faecal incontinence is often caused by constipation and a medical check-up is necessary to establish the cause. Correct diet (or at first, to stop the immediate problem, an enema given by the district nurse) will help to correct the condition. However, there are other causes, such as the effects of a stroke, brain disorder such as dementia, food poisoning (which will be accompanied by vomiting and should be treated as an emergency), drugs, confusion and immobility. As with urinary incontinence, medical and nursing support and aid will be very necessary.

While incontinence is a problem for the sufferer, it can also be a tremendous problem for the carer, and one which is usually anticipated with horror. Perhaps your parent is living with you and you have given her devoted care and attention for many years, either full time or fitting in all your extra duties with a job and/or a family. If she becomes incontinent from one cause or another, it may seem the last straw, something that tries your patience and love to its utmost (see Bridget's story, page 167). It is essential to call upon all the help you can get and to try to take a calm and rational look at the situation so that the work involved is kept to a minimum and you can comfort and reassure your parent as much as possible. She may be suffering from dementia and not realize what is happening, but on the other hand she may be acutely aware of the problem and feel great shame and distress that she cannot control herself and that she is making a lot more work for those who are caring for her.

First of all, your parent's doctor should give her a thorough examination and refer her if necessary to a specialist. All the aids available from a physiotherapist, a district nurse or a health visitor should be called upon. They will be able to tell you how to obtain a commode and teach your parent how to get to it if she is confined to bed. Various other types of appliance are available, and the nurse can advise which would be most useful in your parent's case. She can also advise on incontinence pads and special sheets for the bed, and will help you to arrange it so that it is both comfortable and protected. Do not forget that there is a laundry service available for the bed linen of incontinence sufferers, and the local social services department may be able to supply a home help who can deal with personal laundry for her, if your parent does not live with you.

If your parent is active but still has the embarrassing

problem of incontinence, she may like to consider using special pants (a version for men is also available). The pants, which are made of knitted polyester, are worn next to the body, and outside the pants is a waterproof pouch into which is fitted a specially absorbent incontinence pad. Urine passes through the pants and is soaked up by the pads, which should be changed about four times a day. The pants should be changed daily and washed and dried in between wearings. The pads present the same problems of disposal as disposable baby nappies. Like them, the pads can be torn open and the contents flushed down the lavatory, but the outer part should either be burned or placed in a plastic bag in the dustbin; they would otherwise cause a blockage in the lavatory.

If your parent is wearing incontinence pads which are kept in place by plastic pants, it is important to make sure that she does not become sore as a result. She or you should make sure that she washes the bottom area once or twice a day, drying it thoroughly and protecting it with a silicone barrier cream. The nurse or doctor will advise on a suitable one.

If garments or bedding do become soiled or urine-soaked, they should be soaked in cold water at once, before being washed in the usual way. If there is an offensive smell, there are preparations which can deal with it. Ask at the chemist's; one particular sort is recommended for deodorizing the commode, clothing or bedding.

PARKINSON'S DISEASE

This disease affects the part of the brain which controls muscular movements and it may be caused by narrowing of the blood vessels. But in most cases no specific cause can be found, and it is not an inherited condition.

There are good new treatments these days for Parkinson's disease which can reduce the symptoms, the main ones being tremor, which can affect arms and head, or stiffness of the muscles, including those used in speaking.

The doctor may start treatment or refer the patient to a specialist. Two kinds of drug are usually prescribed; one reduces rigidity and aids the range of movement and the other reduces tremor. They are strong drugs and can produce side-effects. The Parkinson's Disease Society offers support and information for sufferers and their carers. See Chapter 12 for the address.

DIABETES

If this disorder develops later in life, it is usually mild enough to be treated through diet rather than requiring insulin injections. You should suspect it if your parent becomes thirsty and needs to pass water frequently. She may possibly also lose weight suddenly. The illness is caused by failure of the pancreas to produce insulin naturally, insulin being needed to burn up sugar in the body's tissues. The sugar collects in the bloodstream and is eliminated in the urine. If left unregulated, the condition can cause the patient to go into a coma, induced by the accumulation of poisons in the blood.

A low-carbohydrate and sugar-free diet will be suggested by the doctor, and a careful check will be kept on your parent. If she does not respond to diet alone, her GP may suggest drugs for her to take; only as a last resort will she have to have insulin injections. It is important for diabetics to keep their blood-sugar levels stable, and to take the drugs at the specified times. She or you will be advised in detail of the regime she has to follow, and with care she should be able to lead a life which is normal in most respects apart from diet.

You should be on the lookout for certain other ailments connected with diabetes, as the sooner treatment is given for them, the more likely they will be to get better. Your parent may feel extra tired and may find that small cuts and abrasions take a long time to heal (look out especially for cuts on the feet). Her kidneys may also be affected. Bad circulation can cause serious problems, and if there are signs of visual impairment these too could be directly attributable to the diabetic disorder, so however minor the problem may seem, do seek medical advice at once – in a diabetic a small complication may be dangerous if it is not treated very soon.

INDIGESTION

This is very commonly suffered by the elderly. Jane's grandmother was always complaining of 'heartburn' and would usually drink a cup of hot water to make it better. It is a condition which should be investigated medically as it may be due to one of a number of causes. It may signal the existence of a duodenal or gastric ulcer or a hiatus hernia, in which a small section of the stomach protrudes through the diaphragm. If there is discomfort after eating, 'acidity' (characterized by stomach acids flooding up into the throat), pains in the chest, and wind, the latter should be suspected.

Various simple measures can alleviate the discomfort of indigestion, such as eating light meals of easily digested food, whenever possible avoiding bending down, sleeping propped up and not wearing tightly fitting clothes. Smoking and drinking alcohol should be given up if at all possible. Various drugs can also be prescribed to help the pain and make life more comfortable.

CANCER

At any age, the sooner cancer is detected, the more likely it will be that treatment can effect a cure, though as observed earlier, its progress in the elderly is likely to be more protracted and cause less distress than in younger patients. It may be that a specialist would not recommend surgery for your elderly parent, as it might well cause more pain and trauma than the illness itself; it obviously varies with different cases and you and your parent will have to be guided by the experts.

If you suspect the condition, you should encourage your parent to see her doctor without delay, without, of course, alarming her with your own fears. In older people, marked loss of weight and anaemia need investigation, particularly if accompanied by any of the following additional symptoms: cough, pain in the chest, breathlessness, hoarseness and difficulty in swallowing, blood in the sputum; a lump in the breast, puckering of the skin of the breast, a retracted nipple or bleeding from the nipple; pain in the abdomen, diarrhoea and constipation continually alternating over a period of time, black or tarry stools, fresh blood in the stools, constipation, continuing digestive trouble; blood in the urine; bleeding after the menopause; any thickening of the skin or growth or change in colour of moles, particularly with bleeding; a chronic ulcer which refuses to heal; persistently enlarged glands. Of course many of these symptoms could have other causes, and an investigation may very well set your mind at rest.

If your fears are realized and cancer is diagnosed, it will be a difficult decision as to how much to tell your parent, and there is no answer applicable to every case. While many people say they want to know the worst and prepare themselves, this may be something it is easy to say when you are feeling fit, but infinitely hard to take when you are not. You will have to rely on your knowledge of your parent's character together with the doctor's advice and the prognosis. If, for example, the chances of recovery are good, it might be better for your parent to be told so that she can co-operate fully with any treatment prescribed, particularly if she is a woman of strong character and determination. It is a dreadful prospect, if the prognosis is not good, to have to tell anyone that they are under a death sentence, and many people feel that a ray of hope should be left, even in severe cases. Some sufferers ask outright, 'Am I going to die?', but others do not – perhaps because they do not want their worst fears to be put into words or because they know at heart and want to spare whoever is looking after them. Every case is different.

While close family and friends will want to hear the truth, it may be better not to tell more casual acquaintances at first, and to try to encourage your parent to get out and about as much as possible in the normal way, if she still has the strength. You will find that a special diet is prescribed for her and that if she has had hospital treatment various care procedures will need to be kept up when she is at home. You will be able to call on various kinds of aid from the social services department and your parent's GP.

There are many excellent organizations to help sufferers from cancer and their carers, and they can provide help ranging from grants for food, bedding, fares for visiting and convalescence to day and night nursing services and accommodation for sufferers in special homes. Advice, counselling and support can also be given. See Chapter 12 for names and addresses.

Note This chapter and the following one are necessarily brief and by no means exhaustive. Guidelines on nursing, for which specialist literature is needed, have not been included, but readers are recommended to consult an excellent new book, *The Macmillan Guide to Home Nursing*, by Diana Hastings, RGN, RCNT, which contains much valuable advice on lifting and moving, general care of bedridden patients, organizing the sickroom, invalid diets, drugs and treatments, as well as specific chapters on caring for the disabled, mentally handicapped and the elderly, and looking after the dying.

CHAPTER 10

Mental illnesses

Many people who can cheerfully cope with a parent with physical disabilities and problems will admit that the idea of mental illness in him or her is something they dread and would feel quite inadequate to deal with. If the parent cannot respond to normal conversation, becomes confused, repeats himself and makes unreasonable demands over and over again, the strain on the carer and her family can easily take her to breaking point.

It is easy, too, for old people living on their own, without the stimulation of working company and with little incentive to motivate themselves and go out to meet other people, to lapse into a state of acute worry and depression, which can get rapidly worse. The old person may go to the doctor with physical symptoms while really seeking reassurance – a cry for help. The support that the family and social and voluntary services can give can be a lifeline, though these supports are often fewer than they were in the past. Families nowadays tend to be widely scattered and it can require a considerable investment in time as well as money to visit an elderly parent frequently. With country bus services cut, old people are less mobile, less able to go into 'town' to clubs and shops. Fewer of them belong to a religious group than was formerly the case. The social services are very often understaffed and overworked, so unless an old person's problem is very acute, staff may not have time to visit.

This chapter contains brief outlines of some common mental problems and how they can manifest themselves.

CONFUSION AND DEMENTIA
Everyone becomes confused at times – we all know the feeling, perhaps experienced on holiday, of waking up in the dark in a strange room; it can take quite a few seconds to remember where we are and why we are there. We may

feel confused in a crowded supermarket with the 'muzak' going and people jostling around us; sometimes we may find ourselves totally unable to think what we want to buy and just have to stand still and collect ourselves by a great mental effort.

In older people this confusion can become worse as the brain slows up and is less able to make suitable responses. The reason is that brain cells have been lost; this happens throughout one's life, but speeds up as people get older, and brain cells, once lost, are never replaced. Natural decay or mini-strokes (failure of the blood supply to parts of the brain) also bring about loss of cells. It may occur rapidly or be observable over the course of months or even years. If it happens rapidly, the cause may be some disease or even the side-effect of certain drugs, and treatment may bring about relief. A slow deterioration, while it, too, may be triggered by disease, is most likely to be the onset of dementia or Alzheimer's disease. If the cause is constant mini-strokes, the resulting illness is known as multiple infarct dementia. Fortunately most people retain a sufficient number of brain cells to cope adequately and the loss of them is not so severe as to impair their normal functions, although they may slow up to a certain extent. So there is no need to fear that extreme mental impairment will automatically take place if your parent lives to be very old. We have all seen bright old men and women of 90-plus interviewed on television, able to remember their experiences of many years ago and discuss them collectedly and logically.

Another reason why old people can become confused is the deterioration in the efficiency of organs such as the heart and lungs, liver or kidneys. This can result in lack of support to the brain, which in turn will cause it to function less well. It can either be a slow process, or may happen quickly as a result of a sudden illness affecting one of the organs. If the latter is treated successfully, the secondary symptoms should also disappear.

In the early stages, these are some of the symptoms of confusion you should be on the alert for, and which could well benefit from treatment. One of the most obvious is forgetfulness, which may occur increasingly over a period of time. Not being able to remember the right word, getting mixed up over dates and times, getting lost in familiar places or not recognizing friends or relations – all these are signs. If extreme forgetfulness occurs suddenly, it may be an indication of a physical illness which requires immediate treatment.

Associated with forgetfulness is wandering off, and this can be very alarming for the carer. It can happen during the night, as well as by day, the elderly person being found some way away from home in nightclothes.

Another symptom is having hallucinations or fixed delusions. For example, Ian's elderly mother was so sure that burglars were going to break into the house that all her doors and windows were double-locked and bolted in every possible place, a great source of worry to her family as they wondered how they would ever get in to help her if she were taken ill. In the end, they fixed the locks and had the ends of the bolts sawn off when she was out so that she was adequately but not impregnably locked in – a deception which one may deplore but which at least gave her family some peace of mind. Other old people have delusions about money – that they will not be able to pay their way and are terribly poor. We have all heard stories of old people who lived on the kindness of neighbours yet when they died were found to have hundreds of pounds in notes tucked under the mattress.

A lighter story on that theme concerns two brothers, Keith and Austin, who were the only living relatives of an elderly aunt. She did not live with them, but they kept a constant eye on her and often popped in to help her and see she was all right. In one of her rooms were stacks of copies of the *Radio Times* which she would not part with and which they were convinced she would never look at again. When she had to go into hospital for a minor operation, they thought they would take the opportunity to clean and tidy up her house for her, and they started by burning some of the older copies of the *Radio Times*. When they were removing yet another pile to the garden, a £5 note fell out of one of them. Further investigation revealed that all the copies contained paper money – this was her equivalent of putting it 'under the mattress', but not in such an obvious place! It was officious of Keith and Austin to destroy property which their aunt had expressly said she wanted to keep – and they had to pay for their action by giving back to her an equivalent amount of money to that which had been destroyed. But the action of stashing away the money was a symptom on her part of the fixed delusion that she was going to be burgled.

Sometimes elderly people's personalities change. Where they have been clean, tidy and neat, they become increasingly careless about their surroundings and personal habits. They may become unpredictable, take unreasoning dislikes to some members of the family, lose interest in what is going on and fail to eat and sleep properly. Some of these symptoms could indicate depression, so it is necessary to check with the doctor and see whether treatment could help.

In fact, it is most important to alert your parent's GP at an early stage of any of the symptoms and to obtain specific advice from either a psychiatrist or a geriatric specialist. If the problem has a physical cause such as one of the diseases or conditions mentioned above, and if it has been caught early enough, treatment may well be available. The doctor may advise going into hospital, but if your parent has to remain at home and care and treatment look like being protracted, you must make it clear what you can give in the way of care and facilities and what you are not able to do. If there is going to be adequate support from medical sources, and from a visiting nurse and, if necessary, a social worker, you may feel able to manage, but if not, it is essential to let everyone know where you stand.

If the elderly person is living on her own and the problem is not too severe, take a good look at the safety of her environment and make sure that people will be keeping a careful eye on her welfare. If there is no telephone, see that one is installed if at all possible (there may be help available for this – see Chapter 12) and write a card in large, clear letters, with the doctor's telephone number, your own number and a near neighbour's, to pin up near the phone.

Particular care should be taken if your relative has gas appliances in her home. Though undoubtedly cheaper to run than electrical appliances they can, if faulty, or if inadvertently left on for a very long period, prove dangerous, and adequate ventilation is essential wherever gas appliances are used. Never, in your eagerness to exclude draughts, block off all sources of ventilation in any room that is heated by a gas appliance or contains a gas water-heater of any kind.

Make sure all open fires are adequately guarded and leave a fire blanket or extinguisher in a conspicuous place. Buy an electric kettle with an automatic cut-out and put a pan guard round the cooker. Make sure the house is as orderly as possible, to avoid accidents and to simplify the everyday process of living, finding clean clothes, enough crockery and cutlery, and so on.

In more extreme cases of dementia, or if your parent is permanently confused, speak slowly and clearly in short, easy-to-comprehend sentences. It calls for a great deal of patience when a parent forgets family relationships, confuses one person with another, or repeats a statement or asks a question many times during the day. It is no good trying to insist that such-and-such cannot possibly be true, although you should correct errors gently when they occur, as you would with anyone. However, you may find that there are many topics which have to be glossed over, or that it is better to suggest some other activity such as going to make a cup of tea or pick some flowers in the garden if repetition becomes very marked. It will help to focus your parent's attention if you hold her hand when talking to her, and the contact will be reassuring for her. Get rid of outside distractions as far as possible – switch off the television, for instance – so that communication can be more concentrated. Supply as many memory 'pointers' as you can in conversation to identify the friends or relatives you are talking about to your parent: for instance, 'Your niece Dorothy is coming to see you – the one you went to tea with last week.' Help your parent recover her feeling of identity by talking about the family, showing her cinefilms or photos of them, and giving her things to do that she has always enjoyed – embroidery or knitting, perhaps.

Do as much as possible to simplify life for your parent. Make sure, for example, that clothes are easy to put on: trousers and skirts with elasticated waists, plain jumpers which can be worn either way round and loose dresses without belts. If she is living with you, you could lay them out for her in order each day. Many old people do not like to be seen in the bath, although when they become too infirm or confused it is essential that they have help, so try to leave them their independence as long as possible by giving them adequate aids for bathing and using the toilet.

Your parent may be quite active and physically fit yet still have the problem of forgetfulness. It is important not to try to confine her indoors all the time, yet you may worry about her being out alone. Make sure she has a card on her with your name and address and telephone number on it – or that of some other person who can be referred to. And do not be embarrassed if you are out with her and she makes remarks or does things which draw attention to you both. Most people are very tolerant – and many have had similar problems with their own parents or grandparents, or have heard about them from friends.

If your parent is very confused, she may not even recognize the difference between night and day – and this can be one of the most trying aspects for carers who have to keep a job going or get a family off to work in the morning. Try to establish a routine, as far as you are able, with your parent, instituting regular hours for getting up, eating meals, watching television, having visitors, bathing, going to the lavatory, and so on. These activities will form a pattern which is reassuring to the sufferer and will provide a framework within which you too can work. Of course, this is ideal, and there will obviously be breaks, depending on circumstances. Another help in establishing a routine of going to bed at a certain time is to see that your parent, if she is capable of it, goes out for a walk each day so that by evening she is tired and ready to sleep; this is preferable to encouraging too much rest and sleep during daylight hours. A warm drink in the evening (not just before going to bed, but long enough before for the bladder to be emptied before retiring) will also help relaxation.

Any sudden change from familiar surroundings, such as going on holiday, going into hospital or moving house, may suddenly cause confusion which has previously been apparent simply as a slow and gradual deterioration. The condition may still remain, probably less pronounced, when the old person returns home. Seek medical advice and be ready with extra support if necessary.

The carer's attitude is very important when an old person becomes confused, particularly when the situation persists. Try to come to terms with it and, much as it may try your patience, be as matter-of-fact as you can. Do as many practical things to help as possible – taking the sort of measures suggested above will often help you as well as your parent. To recognize a problem and be unable to do anything about it is very wearing and frustrating, but it is essential that you protect your own emotional state and do not become too involved. You will probably feel acute distress that your parent is no longer the person you used to know; but if you can accept the fact that mental decline is taking place and that your memories of an affectionate and caring parent are the true reflection of her personality, not her present state, you should be able to distance yourself a little from the current situation. You will need all the support you can find at this time, none the less.

Physical problems associated with dementia, such as incontinence, are discussed in Chapter 9, and again, routine and the organization for dealing with such a trying problem will be as vital to the carer as the sufferer.

INSOMNIA
Most people find as they grow older that they need less sleep than formerly, though some will, in fact, sleep more. Very often an elderly person will have a few naps during the day and this will of course mean that he or she needs less sleep at night. If your parent is not sleeping well at night, she will probably be reassured by a talk from her doctor. It need not have any detrimental effect to sleep less as one gets older, but worrying about not sleeping can be very demoralizing. The more the old person worries, the less likely she will be to get to sleep, or, if she is consistently waking up early, it may be a sign of depression. Discomfort such as rheumatic pains or in-digestion can also prevent sleep.

Older people who wake up in the night often like to potter about. They do not particularly mind doing this and may be quite relaxed in the knowledge that they can make up sleep during the next day instead. This might, however, be disturbing for the rest of the household, some members of which will probably have to get up and go to work, so it could be a good idea, to prevent your parent from wandering down to the kitchen to make tea or to the bathroom, to suggest that he has a thermos of tea to take to bed with him and uses a commode in his room during the night. If he wishes to listen to the radio, he could use a transistor with an earpiece so that this does not wake anyone else up.

Encourage as much activity as your parent can manage during the day, as this should help to promote sound sleep, and a small milky drink and biscuit in the evening could help to settle him or her down for the night. A warm bed and room will also contribute to relaxation.

Regard sleeping tablets as a last resort; whenever possible try every other means of ensuring a good night's sleep. In any case, if they are prescribed by the doctor, keep a careful eye on the bottle and do not leave it by your parent's bedside. It is very easy to wake in the night and forget whether one has taken a tablet or not.

DEPRESSION

There can be many reasons for depression and one need not be old to be in this state of mind. However, there are more immediate reasons for it in old people, and it may help if you are looking after or visiting a parent to be aware of some of them so that you can lend a sympathetic ear and let her talk it through with you.

Many old people, directly as a result of the death of a friend or more especially that of a husband or wife, cannot help thinking about their own death, which is inevitably drawing near. It is something we can make ourselves forget when we are young, but particularly if the elderly person is living on her own and does not have too much to distract her it may lie heavy on her mind. Unless there is religious belief, there can be no subject more likely to prey on one's mind and spirits than the thought of soon ceasing to exist, although some old people are very philosophical about it.

Isolation and loneliness in themselves can be very

179

depressing and the struggle to manage on a low income and keep up reasonable standards can lower the spirits. Retirement, particularly for men, can also be a powerful depressant. They miss the company at work and the sense of purpose in getting up every day to go to a job. There may sometimes seem little point in getting up at all. Many people find it distressing to have to apply for financial and other help, and to admit that they need the support, however cheerfully given, of family and social and volunteer helpers – loss of independence can be a severe blow to morale. And an erosion of physical health can bring depression in its wake, as can certain diseases.

We all know how annoying it is to be told to 'count our blessings' and this is not the right approach to help anyone, of whatever age, to throw off depression. It is best to try to get your parent to talk about the cause of his unhappiness and to sympathize with it. Louise's father felt that after the death of his wife there was no point in his going on living. For four years he went through the motions of looking after his house, seeing his grandchildren grow up, visiting Louise and her husband, all the things he did while his wife was alive. He lived in a state of continual depression, alleviated by company, but he would certainly have been much worse if he had had no one to talk to. When your parent has talked his fill, try to suggest some distraction, even if it is only a visit to the shops or to a friend's for a cup of tea. There is no one major way to cure depression in the elderly – it has to be a gradual process, with as many kind and sympathetic friends and relatives contributing to it as possible.

Sometimes when the depression is very bad and you or your parent have become worried, you may feel you should seek help from the doctor. If you cannot find out through discussion why your parent is depressed, or if she feels she is losing her mental grip; if she loses interest in life and lapses into an apathetic state; wakes up early when she has been used to sleeping well; loses appetite and weight; and above all if she hints that she has considered ending her life, you should get medical aid. A number of old people do commit suicide, and it is not a threat to be taken lightly.

Physical symptoms can sometimes indicate depression.

Lack of energy or listlessness can both point to it, although they may also be a sign of physical illness. So can constipation, though this, too, may be a sign of eating less or of some other cause. Headache, other aches and pains or minor illnesses can be physical manifestations of depression and it may be very difficult to link them with it. Confusion, too, can be a sign of depression. If in doubt or worried, do consult your parent's doctor. He may want to refer her to a psychiatrist for a more specialist opinion.

Affection and expressions of love can help considerably, and physical shows of love are particularly supportive. Never be afraid to touch your parent, to put your arm round her and hold her hand. Especially if she has lost her husband or partner, these physical displays of love will be comforting for her.

Practical measures to support your parent – for instance, with visits to a day centre or luncheon club or with more assistance in the home – have the double advantage of providing company and assuring your parent that she is not becoming too much of a burden to the rest of the family. Try the social worker (probably with the backing of your parent's GP) or a voluntary organization.

Drugs can be prescribed for depression, but increasingly other treatment is felt to be preferable. Some drugs have unwelcome side-effects. In some cases the person under treatment does not even bother to take them. Therapy is often more lastingly effective and a visit (or several visits) to a psychiatric day hospital could be preferable. There is probably no complete cure for depression – any more than there is for depression in younger people – but if it can be reduced the sufferer can probably be returned to a state where he or she is able, with support, to cope alone.

EXCESSIVE WORRY

Many of the fears that old people have are, unfortunately, only too well founded these days, and if your parent has been a natural worrier anyway all her life, you may well find that her fears grow out of hand. Anne's mother, for instance, is someone who is likely to need care on the death of her husband. She already has a pathological nervousness about being alone in the house when her husband is out, even in daylight, so it will be imperative that she lives with someone when she is widowed. There will be no question of her coping on her own.

Increasing muggings of old people, particularly in city areas, can make some terrified to go out or even to open their doors to anyone, and they are right to be careful. Lalage's mother answered a knock on her door one evening; it was a young child asking if his cat had strayed into her back garden. Having shut the door, the old lady went out into her garden in the dusk to look for the cat. She was jumped on by a gang of young children, knocked to the ground and severely punched and kicked while several of them rushed into her house and stole whatever they could lay their hands on. She recovered in hospital, but was never again the same in health and died a few months later.

For other elderly people, financial problems are the basis of their anxiety; they may dread the arrival of bills or unexpected items of expense which may arise, and feel they are not going to be able to manage on their income.

A natural fear of becoming ill can easily be magnified and the least symptom put down to incipient cancer or heart disease, and such real fears as that of having a bad fall can often lead to almost complete immobility for someone in a really anxious state.

Usually people are true to their temperaments: if they have been worriers when young, they will remain so, but sometimes people change. For instance, if the pressures of working life which have been a burden for many years are lifted, the retired person can become far more relaxed and calm. Joyce's father was headmaster of a village school and was constantly feeling persecuted and unappreciated by the school managers; he was in fact in a state of great anxiety during the latter part of his working life. On his retirement and removal to a seaside environment he became happy and relaxed and thoroughly enjoyed the years he spent there, until the death of his wife, when anxieties again beset him.

If an anxiety state results in your parent talking constantly about it, you should be able to alleviate the worry with practical advice. You could make her home more secure, see if there are benefits available to help with heating costs, visit the doctor with her, and so on. If the worries become so extreme as to be an obsession, you will certainly have to consult her GP or a social worker.

Depression, tension, insomnia, irritability and symptoms such as headaches and aches and pains can all result from excessive worry.

You may find that your parent is more ready to listen to someone from outside the family, particularly someone who represents some 'authority' such as the medical profession, or perhaps the Church. In this case, have a chat with the outside helper first and explain the problem – you may have taken all possible practical measures and still find your parent is anxious and obsessed and can talk about little else but her problem.

Although, again, your parent's GP may feel it better to try to put things right by consultation with a psychiatrist or by discussion, he may be able to prescribe a tranquillizer which could help. As in the case of most similar problems with the elderly, caring and concerned company, given little and often (or much and often if possible), will have a noticeable benefit.

PERSECUTION

The feeling of persecution, that everyone is 'getting at' you in some way, is a close relative to worry and anxiety. Gordon is 79 and living in a cottage that is old and very damp, with water creeping up the walls. He lives downstairs in one room, surrounded by his possessions and no fewer than three electric fires, and of course he worries a lot about his fuel bills, even though he receives help towards them. Well-meaning attempts to re-house him in dry, sound accommodation have got nowhere – he feels that everyone 'wants him out' of his own home where he has lived for many years, and that everyone is in it together, his doctor, social worker and even his friends and family. Again, the only course of action is to talk it through in a rational and friendly way. In Gordon's case, however, it seems likely that he will remain in his damp accommodation until he becomes too ill to cope alone.

NEGLECT

Some people living on their own become very neglectful

of both themselves and their surroundings. This can be a result of mental illness such as depression or confusion, when nothing seems to matter and nothing is worth doing, or the individual in question may be unused to coping for himself or be too lacking in energy to make the effort required for cleaning and washing. Having no 'audience' to appreciate a clean house and good personal appearance can also lead to apathy and neglect – a direct result of isolation. You may have noticed the problem getting progressively worse in your parent and not liked to say anything, but there may come a time when you will have to discuss it with him and try to get professional help to discover the underlying cause, if you are not able to sort it out between you.

Your parent may not welcome the idea of a home help coming in, for example, in case she disturbs his possessions, or he may be ashamed that the house is dirty and he has not been able to keep up his wife's previous high standards; in this case you will have to try to persuade him of the advantages, once the necessity for help has been accepted. If illness is the cause of self-neglect, it is, of course, necessary to consult the doctor without delay, and your parent may be persuaded to do so to oblige you and allay your own fears and worries.

KLEPTOMANIA

This is quite common among the elderly and some well-known people have been implicated in thefts which seemed clearly to indicate a deterioration in their mental rather than their moral state. Many readers will remember the case of Lady Isobel Barnet in recent years, who tragically committed suicide following her trial for shoplifting.

Taking goods without paying for them can also be a result of genuine absent-mindedness, contributed to by the muzak, lights and generally bewildering atmosphere in many supermarkets. Certain drugs, too, can cause confusion and a sense of unreality, leading to the same unfortunate results. A carer should be aware that this can happen, and take every precaution possible to ensure that her parent is not involved in this problem, however innocently. Stores are becoming increasingly inclined to prosecute for shoplifting, and it might be difficult to establish your parent's innocence, however much you yourself know that she was not to blame.

ALCOHOLISM

This problem is especially prevalent among older women, who perhaps tend to drink at home – and alone – rather than in pubs or clubs as elderly men would. Laura found that in the case of her aunt (see Laura's story, page 192), excessive drinking destroyed her appetite for food and nearly killed her; Laura just managed to sort out the problem in time.

In some cases, including this one, it is probably genuine forgetfulness which makes the person drink too much. Laura's aunt just did not remember how much she had had to drink. In others, drinking can begin as a cure for loneliness, and if it is solitary it can quickly become an addiction. Women tend to conceal the amount they are drinking, perhaps by eating strong mints, by refusing company if they have had too much to drink, or by concealing bottles in secret places. They may exhibit behaviour which is not characteristic of them – aggression, sentimentality, volubility or slurred speech. If you suspect your parent is drinking too much, however embarrassing it might be, the problem must be discussed, if only for the reason that, if she is having medication, her doctor should know about it, some drugs in combination with alcohol having potentially dangerous effects. Obviously, if the problem can be admitted to, there are support organizations which can help, and more company from family and friends may go a long way towards helping her to break the habit.

WEAR AND TEAR ON CARERS

The strain imposed on people taking care of parents with some form of mental disorder is terribly wearing. If you are doing it full-time, the irritation and hopelessness may sometimes be overwhelming. If part-time, and perhaps doing a job and/or looking after a family as well, it can be equally mentally and physically exhausting.

It cannot be said too often that adequate breaks and holidays are not just pleasant, they are essential if you are not to crack up. You should therefore be frank with any official bodies and with your own doctor about the problems you are facing and the help you need. If you do not get satisfaction, keep on trying until you do.

ALICE

Both Alice and her husband, Phil, are working full-time — more than full-time, in fact, as they are building up a freelance business and are often still at their desks at 11 at night, having started early in the morning.

One of their greatest personal worries is the health of Alice's mother, who lives 70 miles away from them diagonally across London. Like so many elderly people she is very independent and has lived on her own for many years since the death of Alice's father. In the spring of 1985 Alice began to notice that all was not well — her mother's memory increasingly failed and the smallest happenings confused and flustered her. This was so gradual that Alice just put it down to 'old age' and thought it might be simply a temporary failing, because she wasn't eating enough, or the weather was cold.

'I found it hard to realize that her condition was permanent and progressive,' said Alice, 'but once I did, I increased the frequency of our own visits, alerted neighbours and contacted the local DHSS. Now my mother has twice-daily visits from a home help and a once-a-day visit from a psychiatrist. Of course we go over very regularly, too. Obviously we just make the time — and my mother still wants to go on living in her own place.

'My main reaction is one of sadness. It's like the end of a long era, of being used to having a capable and independent parent. At first I was continuously worried, day in and day out, until I realized just how much of the strain the local social services were able and prepared to take. I must say that no praise I can give is too high for them.

'My mother has had a succession of three DHSS home helps so far — each has been middle-aged, motherly, amazingly gentle and considerate, hard-working, patient, cheerful, caring. I run out of songs of praise. One even came on her off-duty days, Sundays, seven miles to bring clean and aired laundry for my mother, which she does at her own home. So

far, incidentally, we have not approached any voluntary organizations at all.

'We may be lucky in that her area is particularly good as far as social services are concerned, but I think people in our situation often don't realize how much help is available, and perhaps feel guilty or ashamed that they are not spending more of their own time with their relative – and therefore don't seek help. As to financial support, we are not even allowed to pay the DHSS because of my mother's circumstances (help is not based on our ability to pay).

'Every time we go to my mother's house now, to cook her Sunday lunch, I take everything that is necessary, down to salt, cutlery, tablecloth, flour for the gravy, etc. It's quicker and easier than playing hunt-the-thimble with all the tools and appliances she hides. To date we have opened the fridge door and found clean vests and knickers, a toothbrush and facecloth, a dustpan and sweeping brush, a few baking tins and a jar of coffee. In her dressing-table drawer we have found a kitchen sink brush (being used as a hairbrush), teaspoons, floor polish, washing-up liquid (seeping its way into clothes that should be there) and a packet of biscuits. It's like turning out the pockets of a schoolboy's trousers!'

I asked Alice if she had any advice to give to other carers in the light of her experience. 'I think the main advice I can offer,' she said, 'is to be there when needed to help as much as needed, but not to appear to take over completely. Even fairly unable-to-cope elderly people need a sense of dignity and usefulness, particularly someone like my mother who has been so very independent throughout her life.'

BRIDGET

Bridget lives in a fairly large house in a country village a few miles from a bustling market town. She is married with two young daughters, born after she reached the age of 40. For the last two years she has been caring in her own home for her mother, who has Alzheimer's disease. When her mother came to live with them, her younger child was only a year old.

'Before that, my father looked after Mother by himself – they lived about 150 miles from us and my sister, a trained nurse with a good career, lived quite close and popped in for a few minutes to see them every day or two. Until recently, I had no idea of the problem, but working it out, the signs must have started to appear about fifteen years ago, when she became slightly forgetful and confused.

'We got her to go to the local doctor a year or two later as she had become intensely depressed (it took a lot of persuading as she wasn't the sort of person to be always in the doctor's surgery and in fact hadn't visited him for years). I now realize that this was also a symptom, but the doctor just said, "Pull yourself together, Mrs Wilson. There's absolutely nothing I can do for you."

'Looking back, I wonder now how my father coped. No one understood or realized what he was putting up with; we thought he must be exaggerating. My sister used to pop in for such a short time when she visited that the deterioration in my mother's condition wasn't apparent, and when she got much worse, my father out of loyalty and the feeling of stigma attaching to mental illness didn't cry out for help as he was entitled to do. I sometimes think my sister didn't want to see what was going on – and it is very hard to admit that your parent is changing into someone you don't recognize.

'But there must be thousands of elderly couples, many coping desperately as best they can. I think if my experiences can be of any use in persuading the authorities to organize regular informal checks on all their elderly patients, they won't have been in vain. If a health visitor could just call in regularly to see if there are any problems and to offer a face and name to telephone in case of need, it would be most valuable. With hindsight I can understand that my father's phone calls to us were often a cry from the heart, but when we phoned my sister to tell her that he seemed to be in trouble, she would say that she had visited only the day before and everything seemed fine.

'We eventually got him to agree to Mother going to a day centre sometimes, and to their having a home help – but like most old people, he hated the idea of strangers, however well-meaning, coming into his home.'

What finally precipitated the moving of her mother into her own house was the death of Bridget's father, which started off a chain reaction. Her father had cancer and continued to cope with his wife who, by this time, was advanced in her illness and wandering off whenever she could get out. He was losing sleep, not spending enough time caring for himself, and eventually, thought Bridget, he just gave up. He and her *mother visited for Christmas, when all he wanted to do was rest and sleep, so Bridget managed to take her mother out as much as possible. They returned home just after the holiday and her father died on 2 January.*

After that, Bridget took the children and moved to her mother's home for a time to look after her, her husband visiting at weekends. Then she brought her back to her own home, to try to get her used to the house, then returned again to her mother's house. This happened several times. As she said, it was a nightmare. Her children were very small, the younger one just a new baby, and her mother would often get dressed as many as six times in one night and wander into the bedroom where Bridget and the children were, waking up the children and causing Bridget to have to get up and put her back to bed. The house was very dangerous, with gas fires, a gas cooker and an open coal fire, and Bridget was continually on edge wondering if she had remembered to hide the matches or if the gas fire would be switched on during the night allowing gas to escape and suffocate them all.

'At first,' said Bridget, 'it never crossed my mind to have her come and live with us, but it was clear that the situation couldn't go on. We arranged for her to go into a private nursing home at first, but by the end of the third week she was there she was being helped – or rather half-carried – by two assistants to the dining-room. She had been drugged to make life easier for the staff – tranquillizers three times a day, more at night plus two Mogadon tablets. It was then I decided that I would have to have her with us – and I must say that without the understanding and support of my husband, I couldn't have coped over these last two years.

'We are lucky in being able to give mother her own big room, plus a smaller one and a bathroom, but I don't think she knows what the bathroom is for. She won't use a commode, and insists on a chamberpot – when she uses anything at all. I don't think we could possibly manage if we didn't have plenty of space, certainly not with young children.

'One of the most difficult aspects is the hyperactivity which people with this illness display. She was always "escaping" and wandering along the edges of motorways, causing us to have to call the police and spend hours looking for her. I remember one day when I took her and the children shopping, she didn't want to leave the car, and like a fool I forgot to

re-fasten her seatbelt. When we came back, she had gone. I dashed to my husband's office nearby and left the children while he and I looked everywhere for a couple of hours without finding her. Eventually she was spotted wandering along the edge of a busy bypass by a policeman and they went and got her. This is typical of the many, many times she has gone off on her own.

'In the house, I have always had to think one or two jumps ahead and keep an eye on her all the time. The mental strain has sometimes been so intense that I've had to go away to another room sometimes to get a grip on myself and pray (though I'm not a religious person) for patience. With someone in this state, you can't turn your back for a minute – for example, I did a pile of ironing, went to put the ironing board away, and when I came back, the clothes had completely vanished. I found them a few days later in the freezer! You can find anything anywhere – our daughters' wendy-house was found to contain the butter and potatoes! It's all right if you don't want things in a hurry. She had always been used to having a coal fire, too, and this lodges in her mind. We found her laying twigs under our antique table, obviously with a view to lighting a fire, and she will often bring in a shovelful of soil "for the fire". She has an obsession with water and runs the taps all the time if you don't watch it – all that lovely, expensive hot water running down the sink. It's the only thing that gets to my husband – he becomes really annoyed. She will pick the cat up and say it's a hat and try to put it on her head. If you didn't laugh, you'd be in tears half the time.

'At least we have managed to have a really good holiday during the time she has been with us. My sister didn't bother to do anything for fourteen months – she did ring up to enquire how mother was, but never how I was coping. Anyway, she gave up some of her holiday and got in Medicare for the rest of the time so we could have a month in Spain. I think she feels guilty in many ways – particularly for burying her head in the sand and ignoring the onset of the problem as she did.

'The social services locally have been excellent – my father didn't get allowances or help, but we have applied for everything we could claim. At first she went into day care for one day a week, and I'd look forward to being able just to sit down and not have to think of anything, just relax. In fact, I felt that the weight of the world was lifted off my shoulders on the days she went to the centre. After they found how bad she was, they gradually extended the day-care time and now she goes for three days a week and some evenings. We take her and collect her on her return. It was much more difficult to arrange long-distance help when she didn't live with us, and my sister found it difficult to admit to outsiders that we, as a family, needed help. Over the last couple of years, the local services have improved, but one disturbing thing is that at first there was only my mother being looked after with her disease – now there are fourteen people in day care.'

I asked Bridget what was the worst day-to-day problem she encountered. 'I suppose everyone in this situation will give you the same reply,' she said. 'The incontinence is really very difficult to deal with. The washing problem was horrendous and I didn't realize that you could get help with this through the social services. At one point I was using two of the largest-size packets of washing powder a week. Not only were her clothes wet, but the sheets, blankets and even the candle-wick bedspreads. Imagine trying to wash and dry these every day. This is apart from the washing I had for the family, including my toddler and baby. The worst thing that happened was one Sunday when a locum doctor was due to come and see her. As soon as I went into her room in the morning, I knew we had trouble. She had smeared faeces everywhere – over the walls, on the floor, on her bedding and on herself. By 10 o'clock when the doctor came, I was only half-way through getting the mess cleaned up – I think it was an eye-opener for him, as doctors very often don't see the day-to-day problems that carers have to face. It wasn't the first time we'd had similar incidents, including pressing faeces down the wash-basin and into the overflow. Now we have incontinence pads, and these help a lot. But you still have to be on the alert and take her to the commode if you think she may need to pass water or a motion.

'Mainly because of hygiene, because we have young children, I have had to do something I feel rather guilty about. We do now lock her door at night, when we can't keep a continuous eye on her, so that any mess or problem is contained in her own two rooms and bathroom. I feel bad about it, as I don't feel that anyone should be locked in, really, but in a situation like this you have to do the best you can for all members of the family, and the children matter, too.

'Just three weeks ago she had what I'm sure was a stroke, though the doctor didn't agree with me. Anyway, since then she's been off her legs. In some ways it's a lot easier – I no longer feel I have to have eyes in the back of my head, and it's probably no longer necessary to lock the door at night. But in other ways, of course, it's a lot harder – physically harder, I mean. She has to be lifted and moved for everything, but now I can get some outside help for that, which is marvellous. It's still quite a strain, though, as of course I can't expect the district nurse to do everything that's needed and she isn't there much of the time. She's easier to cope with when my husband is around – I suppose she connects him with my father and is more likely to do what he suggests.

'I have to admit that it's no sort of life for my mother – she can't read, converse, do anything at all. She will spend hours tearing up her incontinence sheets and she's totally oblivious to everyone. She doesn't know me or any of the family. She thinks my children are hers, and that my husband is her own. But I wouldn't have come to a different decision, given the time over again. I couldn't have lived with my conscience if we had put Mother in a home. When it comes to the point, though, you don't know how you are going to react. I'd never blame anyone who decided to put their parent into a home. It's everyone's personal decision, and all circumstances and personalities are different.

'I'd just say that if you decide to take over caring for a parent in this advanced state, do make sure you get all the help you can and are entitled to, and don't feel guilty if you feel you are falling short of the standards you have set yourself. We can only do as much as we can, and we owe a duty to our families and ourselves as well as to the parent we are caring for. But I do think there should be an official, but tactful, visiting service which could perhaps prevent situations like my father's. I shall never know what he suffered and put up with for love of my mother.'

LAURA

For the past seven years, Laura and her husband Richard, who are themselves middle-aged, have had continuing problems which are only now beginning to resolve themselves. Laura's health is not good, and both her sons, at the time the problems *arose, some seven years ago, were married and living away.*

'It started with my aunt,' said Laura, 'who lived 35 miles away from our house. She told me at that time that she felt she was not coping as well as she should be, and that the garden, particularly, was proving far too much for her. Knowing she would hate to leave her home, I started to visit her regularly one day a week to do the garden. Gradually over the next months I realized her memory was deteriorating and she asked for help with shopping and other small chores. This continued until about two years ago, when she started to say that she was too old to manage her house. I arranged for her to have a home help, and she had also previously put her name down for a local retirement home. I also found out some addresses, but whenever the subject of giving up the house arose, she said she was not ready to move "just yet". Knowing the trauma of moving would be most upsetting for her, I went along with her reasoning, even though I knew she should not really be on her own.*

'As time went on, I realized she was drinking far too much and hardly bothering to cook and eat (she has always had a very small appetite and was used to alcohol). She fell over once or twice, but fortunately was only badly bruised and broke no bones. Like many people of her age who have always enjoyed excellent health, any mention of getting the doctor to see her was pooh-poohed. But after twice visiting her in two successive weeks when she obviously had not dressed (I did her washing, and there was none), had not eaten (last week's food was still in the refrigerator) and was so weak she could hardly get out of her chair, I felt so worried that I sent for her doctor, much to her annoyance.*

'He said she was not to be left alone any longer. He explained this to her and she agreed to let me take her home. We eventually found an excellent nursing home for her near us (I did feel it would have been wiser for her to be in her own area, but unfortunately there were no vacancies at the time). But at least I can now visit her twice a week, and because of her complete confusion and poor memory she is now settling down.*

'For a few weeks she was very, very difficult and accused me of "kidnapping" her. It was quite understandable she would be dreadfully upset at having to leave her home, but because she was fuddled with drink and very weak, it was* *quite impossible to convince her how desperately she needed help and for someone else to make decisions for her. Once she had had a few weeks at our house with regular food and reasonable amounts of alcohol, she was much more relaxed.*

'So far as my aunt was concerned, we tried not to be hurt by accusations of interference in her life – we knew it was the last thing we wanted to do – and I'd say to other carers, don't be hurt – it is so extremely difficult to convince a confused person that she needs help. In retrospect, there are so many signs of oncoming senility, but they are first of all few and far between and if one has had no previous experience they are often overlooked or joked about.

'Unpaid bills lying about, returned cheques incorrectly made out, cash tucked into library books and unanswered mail in strange places are all signs that something is affecting the old person's normal way of life. Constant repetitions of conversations (one of the most difficult things to bear) and complete inability to remember even important appointments despite constant reminders are all signs. So is inertia connected with previously enjoyed interests. My aunt was an enthusiastic and good bridge-player nearly all her life, but she started to say it was too much trouble to have friends in to play, even though all she had to do was provide coffee, biscuits and drinks. If, as in her case, alcohol is a problem, it is worth pointing out that the person is not necessarily alcoholic, but poor memory means that they really do forget that they have recently had a drink or even had quite a few drinks. Loss of memory is a dreadful problem in so many ways and, combined with confusion, can be disastrous.'

In addition to trying to sort out her aunt's affairs, Laura had to take over the care of her mother-in-law. About two years ago she noticed that her memory was becoming worse and that she, too, was suffering from inertia. She may have been affected by worry over her (second) husband's illness, which was incurable. He lost the power of speech, which made life very frustrating and difficult for both of them.

'I felt so sad,' said Laura, 'that in their old age when they should have been relaxing and enjoying their last years peacefully they should be made so unhappy by physical and mental problems. I started visiting them more frequently and suggested various ways of coping with their problems, helped with the shopping, etc.

194

'*Eventually we realized she was drinking too much alcohol and she became very difficult, aggressive and abusive. Her husband's doctor suggested they sold the house and moved to sheltered accommodation, but they both rejected this idea completely. After some weeks of coping with constant phone calls and answering these distress calls by going to her house to try to calm her, we realized we could not cope on our own, and called in her own doctor. This annoyed her greatly as she was still convinced there was no problem with her health or condition.*

'*Her doctor was most helpful and called in a social worker and health visitor, who were wonderful. After some weeks of calls and long conversations with the helpers, family consultations with her husband's family and us, we were eventually all able to persuade her that the alcohol was affecting her and she did try to cut down. For the last few weeks she has succeeded admirably.*

'*She also saw a psychiatric doctor who has diagnosed senile dementia and even though her aggressive moods have stopped, she is very, very confused and her memory is very unreliable. Apparently she can only deteriorate and it will eventually become necessary for her to be in hospital, but she does seem to be in remission at present.*

'*The last months have been incredibly exhausting, both mentally and physically, even though she has not been under our roof – how people cope with someone with these problems living with them I just don't know. One feels so helpless, even though one is constantly trying to cope. A social life has been impossible, as her distress calls were obviously so erratic I felt I had to be available to go to her at a moment's notice. I felt I could only give part of my attention to her as I was trying to help my aunt as well, and had problems with my own health. Fortunately I am blessed with a marvellous husband (her son), who has a sense of humour and who helped whenever he could, usually managing to find the funny side of most situations to lighten some of the really bad moments.*

'*One of the most difficult things I found was the feeling that I was removing my mother-in-law's right to make her own decisions, even though she was often quite incapable of doing so. I had to keep reminding myself that it was necessary to do this and not to worry about it. It is most important to check that your relative is actually coping with her financial affairs*

– paying bills, keeping building-society books, bank books, etc. in a safe place. Quite by accident I one day discovered she had a great deal of money in various places in the house. This was after she had told me she went to the bank regularly to pay in money, which she could not have done for months. I immediately had to collect it all up and go and pay it in because I knew she would not get round to it. Because of confusion and poor memory, you can never rely on anything you are told – check up on everything. *It took me a long time to realize this.*

   'I would say to other people in the same situation as I was with my aunt and mother-in-law, do ask for as much help as possible as soon as you realize there is a problem and don't try to cope alone for too long. We had excellent help from the DHSS, doctors, and so on, and even now when things have quietened down the health visitor still calls on my mother-in-law once a fortnight. I've also found Help the Aged very good – they have lists of sheltered accommodation, and our local council has a voluntary service, Homefinding for the Elderly. I think it would be most useful to have some form of group help in each area, just as young mothers do when they want to organize a babysitting circle. A phone call could bring a helper to grannysit for an hour or two to relieve the carer for a bit so that he or she could have some private time to themselves. This would apply more, of course, to people who actually had an elderly relative living with them.'*

CHAPTER 11

Coping with a death

Even if your parent has been ill for some time and you have mentally prepared yourself to expect his or her death, it is always a sadness when it does happen. The death may on the other hand have been unexpected and come as a shock to you. For many people the death of a parent is their own first experience of dying, a subject which of recent years has taken the place of sex as something one does not talk about, and the reality can be quite overwhelming.

You may, of course, feel that the parent you used to know died some time ago, if illness and mental impairment have changed him/her in the last stage of life; or you may be thankful, if he or she was in great pain, that the suffering has ended. A moving book by an American writer, Betty Rollin, called *Last Wish* (Viking) describes how her mother, after long and painful experience of cancer, knowingly took an overdose of drugs to end her suffering and die with dignity. Betty is with her as she dies: 'I stumble backwards, collapse into a chair and with both hands clamped over my mouth, I sob. I sob heavingly, but not for long. Because when I look up and see how still she is, I know that she has found the door she was looking for and that it has closed, gently, behind her.'

If you know your parent is dying and she is still at home, you will need as much support as you can get while sustaining, as far as possible, the normal life of the family. All the members of the family will, of course, be under considerable stress, but everyone should make a conscious effort to keep calm and reduce the tension that will inevitably be in the air. If the parent is in hospital and desperately wants to get home – a very understandable feeling if she feels that the end is approaching – you have a very difficult decision to make. She may still need considerable nursing, and of course there is no knowing how a patient may rally, but most families want to fall in with last wishes if they possibly can and will be uncertain what to do for the best. Perhaps the best course of action is to talk to the doctor at the hospital, or the sister in charge of the ward, and ask his or her advice, explaining the circumstances at home and any other relevant details. An unbiased opinion from someone not emotionally involved is always worth having.

Another difficulty is whether to tell the elderly person that he or she does not have much longer to live. Again it will be necessary to talk to the doctor, in the light of your knowledge of your parent's character, which will be better than his. For some old people, knowing that death is imminent is a terrible thing to come to terms with, but others would prefer to know so that they can, as it were, put their spiritual – or temporal – house in order, especially if they are religious or if, on the other hand, they need to make arrangements for the disposition of their estate. There can be problems if an old person is told prematurely that she has not much longer to live and then unexpectedly rallies.

It is just as well to be prepared for the question 'Am I going to die?' before it is asked. It can often catch relatives off guard, and if it is asked of different members of the family, disturbingly different answers may be given. If the parent is told when she is calm and perhaps feeling a little stronger, there is no guarantee that the information will not make her feel overwhelmingly worried and miserable on a day when she is feeling worse, so it is necessary to be very sure that she does, in fact, really wish to know the truth and can cope with it.

Carers will, of course, feel a desperate desire to do everything possible for a dying parent. Apart from providing a warm, comfortable and peaceful environment, it is essential to see that she receives adequate medication to control pain and give her peace of mind. All those involved should be careful of conversations in her presence as, although she may appear to be sleeping or in a coma, people in this state can be quite aware of what is going on and hear comments – we all know how quickly we pick up remarks in which our own name is included. So do not speak about her, but *to* her, calmly and gently.

You may find over the final few weeks that her attitude changes towards you and other members of the family. The change may take the form of becoming difficult and demanding, or of withdrawing into a world of her own – or anything in between. Try to realize that this does not imply any criticism of you and your care, but is a reaction to illness and a preparation for handing over the business of living to others and for leaving the world behind.

If you or your parent is religious, now is the time to ask for help and support from the Church or other religious organization. This can help enormously at such a critical time, though anyone, however religious, may dread the actual moment of death, particularly if he or she has never been at a deathbed before. Many people find, however, that it is so peaceful that their fears were unfounded. When the spirit has departed, it is strange but true that there really is 'nothing there'. The vital spark that made the person has gone; only the empty shell of the body is left behind.

If your parent dies at home, you must call the doctor, who is responsible for issuing a death certificate. He will be able to recommend someone or send a nurse to lay the body out (that is, wash and prepare it for burial). In the unlikely event of his not having seen the patient for more than 14 days, the local coroner must be informed of the death and will decide whether an inquest should be held. If the old person dies in hospital, the doctor in charge will issue the certificate.

The death must be registered as soon as possible at the office of the Registrar of Births, Deaths and Marriages within whose boundaries your parent died. This should be done within five days in England and Wales and within eight days in Scotland. A copy of the entry and a disposal certificate together with one free copy of the Certificate of Registration of Death are given to whoever registers it. If you need extra copies for insurance or other purposes there is a small charge. If an inquest has to be held, the death cannot be registered until the outcome is known.

The undertaker will take over the funeral arrangements from this point onwards, but if you wish your parent to be cremated note that the death certificate will have to be signed by two doctors, not just one, and that other forms will need to be completed. The undertaker will give you much help and advice and can arrange for an announcement to be put in the paper, book the funeral date, order flowers, and so on. The body may either remain at home, if practicable, or may be taken to a chapel of rest by the undertaker. Funeral costs can be high, so it is a good idea to ask the undertaker for a written estimate, once the matter has been discussed.

Although many people find it a distasteful subject to contemplate before the event takes place, there are ways of paying in advance towards funeral costs, which can relieve the burden when the time comes. The Co-operative Funeral Society, for instance, has what seems like a remarkably advantageous scheme for making an advance payment or series of payments towards the cost of a funeral. The amount paid is set against the cost of a funeral provided by the society. Vouchers to the value of 50 per cent of the amount paid are issued in the meantime which can be used right away to purchase items from the Co-op – not its food departments, but any other: for instance, a Funeral Service Certificate to the value of £200 would entitle the holder to spend £100 on clothing, bedding or other items. You can pre-pay any amount in multiples of £50. Further details are obtainable from your local Co-operative Society.

Although a Death Grant from the DHSS has long been available for many people, new plans have been put forward, coming into effect in spring 1987, to replace the grant with financial aid for those in or out of work who are responsible for paying for a funeral but are unable to meet its cost. Ask for details at your local DHSS office or branch of Age Concern.

Once the funeral is over, there will be many loose ends to tidy up. If you are your parent's executor you will have to deal with the will, if your parent made one, and obtain probate through a solicitor, sort out bank accounts, insurance policies, and so on. If you need advice, your local CAB or Age Concern office will be helpful.

It will also be necessary to go through your parent's personal belongings, including clothes; this is a task much better done with someone else to help you, because more than anything these possessions will remind you of the person who has died, and will seem very pathetic. If there are items you or the rest of the family do not want, many charities will be glad of them to sell for their funds – perhaps there is one in which your parent was particularly interested. If not, remember such organizations as the Salvation Army, which can always put items of clothing, bedding and so on to very good use.

Having to deal with so many practical matters can help one over the first days when someone dies, but when everything is done the sense of loss often returns. Whatever the circumstances, people will often try to comfort the bereaved with such well-worn comments as 'A happy release' or 'She's had a good life', and of course they are well-meaning. But essentially you will have to find your own comfort and work through your emotions over a period of time. You may feel that there was more you could have done when your parent was alive, or reproach yourself for moments of impatience or irritability. Most people have these feelings – they are entirely natural when someone has died, as are depression and fear, unhappiness and deep grief. Do not try to suppress what you feel, but talk about it with family or friends; repression can be very bad for you and have long-term physical effects such as weight loss, loss of appetite and lethargy. You may have been under extreme strain, both mental and physical, while looking after your parent, and the relief when it is over often causes guilt that such relief should be felt. All these feelings are very common and should be admitted to someone close to you to help alleviate them. Gradually the bereavement will recede into the past, though most people say that it takes at least six months to begin to recover from the death of a close relative. With many people it is longer than that. When the period of mourning and grief has gone by, one begins to remember again all the happy times and the unhappiness fades away. Good memories, after all, are the best memorial anyone could have.

HELEN

Helen's 84-year-old mother was living in her own home, shared by Helen's brother and his wife. She was a very independent old person who, if she felt unwell, would hesitate to mention it and would not admit that anything was wrong with her, particularly as she knew that Helen and her husband were in the process of establishing two new restaurants and were working fourteen or more hours a day.

However, unknown to Helen and her brother, a problem was building up. When Helen visited, it was not apparent that anything was wrong, and her brother was too close to the situation to notice the slow deterioration in his mother. She gradually started to behave oddly, behaviour which was just put down to her 'getting older', but when Helen phoned, a few weeks before Christmas, to make arrangements for the holiday, her mother sounded so strange that she rushed over immediately and found her, as she put it, 'in a very bad way'. Helen did not wait until Christmas, but took her mother back with her immediately, feeling that it was her turn to look after her as her brother and sister-in-law had been doing so for a long time.

At first she did not realize the extent of the problem. But her mother had two falls and hurt her head, and began to exhibit the beginnings of dementia. She developed a Jekyll-and-Hyde personality, being her own normal, cheerful and witty self during the day, but going, as Helen put it, 'quite out of her mind' at night. As they were afraid of her falling downstairs in a strange house in the dark (especially as her eyesight rapidly deteriorated), Helen and her husband rigged up a kind of gate at the top of the stairs, and would find her time after time throughout the night crying and calling for help. They would put her back to bed, calm her and say it was time to go to sleep as they had to be up and at work in the morning, only to find the same situation repeating itself after an hour.

Of course they consulted the doctor, who seemed, according to Helen, to be mainly concerned with her mother's physical problems. However, he did diagnose the onset of dementia – as did the geriatric department of the local hospital. Neither did anything about her mother's sleeplessness, either to help her or to give a respite to Helen and her husband.

On Christmas night, when all the family were at Helen's, her mother had the most violent attack of all, which alarmed everyone and certainly alerted the whole family to her state. With Helen being so busy, it was clear that this state of affairs could not be allowed to continue, and Helen and her husband employed a private nurse to be with her mother all day, as she certainly could not be left. She was fine for spells – just as normal – but then her condition would deteriorate, and although she was not incontinent, she could not dress herself, for example, without help. But in the evening, one or other of them had to stay with her, which posed enormous problems as far as their business was concerned, and of course left the same difficulty of night waking for them both to cope with.

The problem was totally unexpected and they were quite unprepared for it. They rang a number of people for advice and found various organizations very helpful, notably Counsel and Care for the Elderly. But of course there was no time to make contact with support groups of other carers, something which, Helen says, looking back, would have been of the utmost help to her.

Having decided that the only solution was to find a good residential home which would take Helen's mother, the couple looked at a number locally. They were horrified by some of them, where rows of old ladies sat looking into space, apparently completely apathetic and unoccupied. They eventually found a very small private home which took six or eight elderly ladies and gave excellent individual attention and care.

'It was very harrowing,' recalls Helen, 'as she kept saying, "You won't send me away, will you?" all the time. I felt terrible, but I had to try to distance myself and look at the situation dispassionately. Our business employed fifty people and was a very personal one which relied on my being there. I had to take a cold decision as my mother clearly needed 24-hour-a-day care and neither of us was getting any sleep at night. I should have thought that this problem must be so common that doctors would be used to dealing with it and supplying suitable sedatives, but in my experience they don't seem to take into account the family situation at all.

'Eventually my mother did go into the home, and the staff there advised us not to visit for a week, so that she would settle down (I gather this advice is often given to carers). Looking back, I'm not at all sure that it was right in my mother's case; she had lucid intervals when she must have thought that we had just put her away and abandoned her.

Her state obviously preyed on her mind and she would often cry and say, "What shall I do? I don't know what to do." I'm afraid that her health failed – she had no resistance. After a short time in the home she developed pneumonia and was taken to hospital, where she died the following February.

'I have felt dreadfully guilty ever since as I think she just gave up, but I don't think I could have come to any other decision given the situation and our other commitments. Everything happened so quickly and at such a busy time of year that we didn't have the time to get ourselves prepared either mentally or physically. Perhaps the best advice is to think ahead – this is the sort of situation which could happen to anyone, and it is best to have contingency plans, even if they are only in a rudimentary form.

'Many of my friends are now getting into the age bracket when something similar could happen to them. I'll certainly pass on the addresses of the organizations which help carers. You never know when they will be needed.'

CHAPTER 12

Help directory

This chapter contains further details of many of the organizations and services mentioned elsewhere in this book.

PROFESSIONAL ORGANIZATIONS
Social services department
This is a local government service supervised by the local council and will help elderly people with the day-to-day running of their lives. Among the department's responsibilities are services for old people leading an independent life in their own homes, and these include:

- meals-on-wheels service, which generally provides meals on a five-day-a-week basis
- lunch clubs and day centres, to which old people are taken often in transport provided by the department
- home helps
- installation of a telephone and financial help with the rental charges
- supplying and licensing of television and radio
- laundry service for linen where appropriate
- various aids to make the home more manageable for the elderly.

The department also provides a comprehensive information service about what it offers and also about any other services which can help the elderly in any way, so if your parent is thinking of moving, it would pay to check beforehand on what is on offer under different councils.

It is also responsible for providing residential old people's homes and for supervising private or voluntary homes. Under the department come the social workers who have to make the service work and decide who is eligible to receive what help. They also help relatives and the old people themselves with advice and information;

they have to be skilled and flexible in their assessment of various problems and offer solutions as far as possible. Social workers can often help in sorting out family difficulties – for instance, if one member feels she is having to do too much for the elderly person – and in helping those involved to come to a decision over whether the person in question should at last be admitted to a home. A frank discussion with someone professional who is not emotionally involved can often help to clarify everyone's ideas and arrive at the best possible solution (even though you will probably have to come to terms with the fact that there may not be an ideal one).

Social worker Anyone can consult a social worker direct. Either phone the social services department or write, with a concise description of your problem. (Experienced carers say writing is better.) Involve your parent if at all possible. You will be given an appointment and can then discuss all aspects to see whether the social worker is the best person to help, what she (or he) can do – or if not, who would be the best person or organization to consult. In case of need, there is an emergency service you can ring up.

Home help service The home help organizer is responsible for a given area and for allocating home helps, using her judgement as to cases of greatest need. The amount of home help available varies from area to area and sometimes, however much the organizer would like to provide help, she simply may not have enough staff available. The home help not only helps with the shopping, housework and preparing food, she is a valuable person to keep an eye on an old person and see that all is well. The organizer decides how much time can be given and how much the old person should pay, and this of course will entail a discussion of her finances. Heavy work and nursing care are not usually provided by the home help.

Scottish Home and Health Department
For its leaflet *Help for the Handicapped in Scotland* write to the Department at St Andrews House, Regent Road, Edinburgh EH1 3DE.

MEDICAL SERVICES
General practitioner

A good doctor is a priceless asset, not only to an elderly person, but to you if you are a carer. Not only will he diagnose and treat and, if necessary, recommend hospital care, but in a group practice he may well have links with an occupational therapist who makes domestic visits, and with a social worker.

Try not to be too critical of a doctor who does not visit regularly if there seems to be no specific need, or whose receptionist asks if the sick old person can possibly make it to the surgery – many practices, especially in cities, are heavily overloaded. If an old person is chronically ill and needs to visit regularly, perhaps a friend can take her by car, or there may be a voluntary driving service linked with the practice. If she falls ill and a home visit is really necessary, try to phone the doctor before 10 am to arrange the visit – though of course if there is an emergency this will not be possible.

If there has to be a night visit, you may find a deputy comes instead of your parent's own GP. In that case, be ready with all the information he will need, as he will obviously not be so familiar with the case.

Sometimes relatives disagree with the receptionist on the urgency of a required visit. Try not to insist if the problem can wait, but if you really think it is urgent and you are not getting anywhere, ask to speak to the GP so he can decide. It may sometimes seem to elderly people that those who make the most fuss get the most attention, but in fact it is very difficult to judge other people's needs, and this decision must ultimately be made by the GP, who is trying to do a very exacting job. The old days of social visiting and 'bedside manner' which your parent may have been used to and which she probably looks back on with nostalgia are over; in return, we have greatly improved drugs and treatments and, by and large, efficient, kind, effective care from our medical services.

If you or your parent is really dissatisfied with the GP, it is possible to change doctors and go to someone else. If your parent is moving to a different area, she will certainly need to find a new doctor. Large post offices or public libraries hold a medical list of all local GPs. You can find out, as well as names, addresses and phone numbers, whether an individual doctor works on his own or in a group practice, what his consulting hours are and whether he has an appointments system. If possible, try to talk to local people about their doctors and see what their opinion is – though unfortunately the 'best' doctors usually have the longest list of patients. Another thing to think about is where the surgery is in relation to the home. It is also necessary to check whether your chosen doctor can accept your relative on his list. If there is no room on any local GP's list, it will be necessary to contact the Family Practitioner Committee about it.

If your parent has moved within her own district, she will probably want to remain with her family doctor. This is usually no problem. But if she moves away, even a little way out of the district, the GP can ask her to find another doctor. If she goes into residential care in the same district, she can continue with her own GP, even if another one is the normal visiting doctor for the home.

Registering with a new doctor entails handing in the parent's medical card to the receptionist at the surgery. If it has been mislaid, all details should be sent to the Family Practitioner Committee, including the name and address of the previous GP, so that a new card can be made out. If your parent is staying with you temporarily, your own doctor can treat her if necessary. It is a good idea to register her temporarily – the registration lasts for three months – and during that time she then becomes, to all intents and purposes, one of your doctor's own patients.

Health visitor
There is usually a health visitor attached to a group of general practitioners; she will also be part of a team of health visitors who will stand in for one another when the need arises. A qualified nurse who has taken an extra year of training, she will know what services are available, both voluntary and professional, and how you or your parent should apply for them. She can keep an eye on the old person and is trained to recognize any change or deterioration in her mental or physical health – and will alert the GP (this is especially valuable if you do not live nearby and are unable to visit frequently).

She can also help in any discussions between you and your parent to sort out practical and emotional matters. Her job and that of the social worker overlap to a certain extent, but if the old person were to want one of the social services department's services, the health visitor would not be empowered to provide it – she would have to ask a social worker to process the application, if she considered it appropriate. Health visitors do not do any physical nursing, unless they live in country districts, where the job of health visitor may be combined with that of district nurse.

If you want to enlist the services and visits of a health visitor, get in touch with your parent's GP. You may find he has already asked the health visitor to call. If not, you will be told when and how to contact her.

District nurse
The district nursing service consists of qualified nurses and nursing auxiliaries under their supervision. District nurses usually work as part of a domiciliary team (one that attends on homes rather than, for example, hospitals), so that although they may also be part of a primary care team, their work can be covered every day of the week. For this reason, it may be that your parent will not always be visited by the same nurse.

The qualified nurses will carry out the more skilled tasks, such as giving injections and being responsible for medication, while the auxiliaries will help with washing, dressing and other general care. If your parent needs to be helped into bed, requires an evening injection, etc., there is also an evening service available. You can telephone to ask a nurse to call, or ask your parent's GP – or he may have asked her already. How many times she will visit will depend on the needs of the patient, how busy the service is and how many relatives live near and can help. If your parent is living with you, visits from a nurse may be your lifeline, especially if the old person is very sick or disabled. Not only can she help you with heavy tasks like lifting, bathing and toileting, but you will have someone to discuss your problems with and give you support, as well as your parent.

If you or your parent has private insurance, you may

find that some help with private nursing is available through this. Private nursing is very expensive, but you may be able to find a friend or neighbour with nursing training who could give you a hand if you came to some arrangement.

Occupational therapist

An occupational therapist plays a valuable and positive role in helping a newly disabled relative (perhaps she has had a stroke, for example) to come to terms with her disability and show her how to help herself and adapt. To master again the art of dressing herself, taking a bath, doing the housework and so on may be a slow process, but professional advice can help her to feel that it will again be possible. If progress is not satisfactory or too much difficulty is encountered in restoring movement, the therapist may recommend a mechanical aid or for some adaptation to be made to the home. Occupational therapists who are based in hospitals can pay a home visit to see if there is any way the home environment can be made easier for the patient when she is discharged. They may then, if necessary, refer her to a domiciliary occupational therapist who will continue visiting.

It is a good idea to speak to the occupational therapist who is looking after your parent so that she can show you what she is doing to help her to become independent, and how you can help. If you have any anxieties about how your parent can adapt and cope, once she is back in a domestic situation, you can ask her this too.

If you can talk through a situation with your parent and the occupational therapist, in the event of difficulties arising at home, you will find that there are probably good practical solutions. The more you can help your parent to help herself rather than your doing too much for her, the less frustrated and helpless she will feel. As in looking after a toddler, it may be much easier, quicker, cleaner and more convenient to do things yourself – but it really does not help the toddler. And the psychological effect of being treated as helpless and dependent when you have led a full and active life can be very detrimental to an old person's recovery. So use all the support you can get to rehabilitate your parent just as much as possible.

Physiotherapist, osteopath and chiropractor

Most physiotherapists work in hospitals, although in some districts a service exists for visiting in the home. The physiotherapist will assess the disability or loss of function resulting from your parent's illness (it could be arthritis, a stroke, or whatever) and treat this, perhaps with massage and manipulation, and by motivating the patient to try gradually to help herself, become more mobile and more active. It is possible to have physiotherapy on a private basis, but the practitioner will probably want a note from the GP before starting treatment. The cost can add up, so it is well worth checking what is available on the NHS before commencing.

Osteopaths and chiropractors are not part of the NHS, although reputable ones are highly trained and well qualified. Many people with bad back problems consult them and they are often able to relieve such conditions as sciatica, lumbago, pains in the upper spine, and so on. Not all doctors are in favour of osteopathy, but a well qualified osteopath or chiropractor will assess a patient's condition and, if he cannot help, recommend that the patient returns to his own GP for treatment. Occasionally you will find an osteopath who is also a qualified physiotherapist.

It pays to ask around for personal recommendations, but if you cannot find a friend with any advice to offer, you can consult the local *Yellow Pages* directory. But be careful. People who are not qualified can set up as chiropractors or osteopaths. For the names of qualified people in your area, write to the British Chiropractors Association, 5 First Avenue, Chelmsford, Essex CM1 1RX; or, for osteopaths, to the General Council and Register of Osteopaths Ltd, 1–4 Suffolk Street, London SW1Y 4HG. (The designation 'M.R.O.', Member of the Register of Osteopaths, is legally protected on behalf of its members.)

Psychiatrist

If mental problems arise in your elderly parent, your doctor may want to get specialist advice from a consultant psychiatrist, not only to find out exactly what is wrong, but to be able to administer the best treatment and to find out whether it would be advisable to put the old person in hospital for a time. Most hospitals of any size will have a psychiatrist who specializes in such problems, known by the imposing name of psychogeriatrician. Careful assessment is needed at the outset to discover the physical or social causes of the mental deterioration and recommend treatment. Sometimes the psychiatrist will make a home visit; alternatively, your parent may be admitted to hospital for a time for observation.

Chiropodist
Treatment for feet is available on the NHS, either in a clinic or health centre, or, less often, on a home visit. The service is however not very extensive and there tend to be long waiting lists, so it may be advisable to consult a private chiropodist if it can be afforded. Make sure, if you get a name from *Yellow Pages*, that the chiropodist you choose is properly qualified and has the letters SRCh (State Registered Chiropodist) after his (or her) name, which guarantees that he has had a three-year training and is insured.

OTHER OFFICIAL SOURCES OF HELP
Citizens' Advice Bureau
This is an invaluable service, offering help in many areas and particularly in providing advice on and addresses for the right people to consult on specialized problems.

Department of Health and Social Security
Anyone taking over the care of an elderly parent will find it well worth visiting the local DHSS office early on to find out exactly what is available in the way of state financial help, both for the old person and for you, as carer. A number of well set out leaflets are obtainable, from DHSS Leaflets, PO Box 21, Stanmore, Middlesex, HA7 1AY, the DHSS Health Services Branch at HS4C, Hannibal House, Elephant and Castle, London SE1 6TE or your local DHSS office. These will repay careful study. Unless you have a lot of time to spare, it is advisable to try to make an appointment to talk to someone at your local DHSS office, as queuing can consume an entire morning. See Chapter 8

for more details about pensions, benefits, etc. and for information on the individual leaflets.

Electricity, gas and solid fuel
Local showrooms and offices should all be able to help with advice on the best types of equipment, ways of economizing with heating, insulation, grants available, and so on. Look out for leaflets, too, at the local Age Concern office. The Electricity Council produces a useful leaflet, *Making Life Easier for Disabled People*, in conjunction with the Disabled Living Foundation, which is full of tips and suggestions for equipment of all kinds, and its siting. A range of leaflets under the general heading 'Electricity and You' is available from electricity board showrooms, free of charge, covering many subjects including 'reading your meter', 'how to make the most of electricity' and 'advice to elderly people'. Useful leaflets from the Department of Trade cover the subjects of furniture and fire and nightwear and fire – both very relevant to the elderly and their carers. They are available from the Department of Trade, Consumer Safety Unit, Room 302, 10–18 Victoria Street, London SW1H 0NN.

Other useful addresses
Solid Fuel Advisory Service, Hobart House, Grosvenor Place, London SW1X 7AE (its booklet *All About Keeping Warm* is well worth obtaining). Local addresses are obtainable from telephone directories or *Yellow Pages*.

Domestic Coal Consumers' Council, 2 Bunhill Row, London EC1Y 8LL

The Royal Society for the Prevention of Accidents will offer advice on making your parent's home safer. It produces two booklets of general interest: *Safety in Retirement* (60p) and *The Home Safety Book* (60p). Contact the Resources Officer, Home Safety Division, RoSPA, Cannon House, The Priory Queensway, Birmingham B4 6BS.

Court of Protection
(See page 140.) Write to the Court regarding Enduring Power of Attorney and Receivership at 25 Store Street London WC1 7BP, or telephone 01-636 6877.

VOLUNTARY ORGANIZATIONS

Fortunately for anyone with problems concerning elderly parents, there are many, many kind-hearted people with a little time to spare to lend a hand and many excellent voluntary organizations geared up to help old people and their carers.

People are often ready to offer a lift to the doctor's or dentist's, come in from time to time to sit with an elderly person or do shopping when they go to get their own. It may not always be possible for them to help on a regular basis, but even occasional help can relieve the strain. Usually a volunteer will not want payment, though you could offer to pay for petrol or bus fares if cost has been incurred, but the person in question may appreciate a donation being made to a local charitable organization in which he or she is interested.

If you or your parent has no direct help, such as a neighbour or official help from the social services, or even if you have, and could use more, you should get in touch with one of the local voluntary organizations such as the Council for Voluntary Service or Age Concern, explain the problem and ask their advice. They will know the best people to help: it might be a student organization, school community service group, WRVS, Good Neighbour Scheme or the Lions, among many others.

Below is a brief outline of some of the organizations or groups you may find locally and how they can help you. It is by no means an exhaustive list, so do check in your own area as there are probably others in your own community with which you can get in touch.

Age Concern

There are many local branches of this widespread organization – consult your local telephone directory. It exists to provide advice, information and help for all elderly people and their carers. If you need advice on financial or housing problems, or to find out about work, recreational and educational opportunities for your parent, or to know where the luncheon clubs or day centres are, or how to get in touch with transport schemes – to give just a few examples – your local Age Concern office should be able to help. Local offices stock a wide range of helpful leaflets and produce an excellent book, *Your Rights for Pensioners*, which costs 70p at the time of writing.

Services available will naturally vary in different parts of Britain: in Norfolk, to take one example, Age Concern Norwich produces a booklet in which much of the information refers to all pensioners, though some is specifically for those living in the City of Norwich. In addition, for those living outside the City, there are several local committees which form part of Age Concern, Norfolk. Both groups are part of the National Age Concern movement, which has its headquarters at Bernard Sunley House, 60 Pitcairn Road, Mitcham, Surrey CR4 3LL (tel: 01–640 5431). The address for Age Concern Scotland is 33 Castle Street, Edinburgh EH2 3DN; for Age Concern Wales it is 1 Park Grove, Cardiff CF1 3BJ.

Alzheimer's Disease Society
This national society gives information, support and advice to people caring for sufferers from dementia. For the address of your local group, write to Bank Buildings, Fulham Broadway, London SW6 1EP.

The Association of Carers and **The National Council for Carers and Their Elderly Dependants** both exist to help and improve the quality of life for carers and their parents or other dependants. Not only do they offer support and practical help with, for example, names of local homes for old people so that carers with no other means of help can have a holiday, sitting services, and so on, but they publish books and leaflets which are well worth consulting. One is the *Help at Hand* booklet, which costs £1 inclusive of p. & p. (for non-members) and is available from the Association of Carers, First Floor, 21–23 New Road, Chatham, Kent ME4 4QJ, as are membership details. The address of the National Council for Carers and Their Elderly Dependants is 29 Chilworth Mews, London W2 3RG. Please send an s.a.e. with your request for information. (See also Chapter 2.)

BREAK
This organization exists to give a holiday to handicapped children or older people so that their carers can also have

some time off. It can only take a limited number of elderly people on special weeks set aside during the year, but it is completely equipped to care for the profoundly handicapped, including demential patients and the incontinent. The cost of a week's holiday was £126 (in 1986), which included full board, day and night care and a recreational programme. Places are not available for elderly people during July, August and September or during the Christmas and Easter school holidays. Generally the carer would bring her parent to the BREAK centre before going off on her own holiday, but in certain cases it might be possible to arrange an escort for the parent to and from the centre, at an extra charge. Special need is BREAK's main concern, and it gives sympathetic consideration to any genuine problem. Write to The Director, BREAK, 20 Hooks Hill Road, Sheringham, Norfolk NR26 8NL or discuss your problem with Mrs Judith Davison, on Sheringham (0263) 823170. Incidentally, friends of BREAK raise money all over Britain as the organization has no government grant.

British Association of the Hard of Hearing
There are local self-help groups for people who are hard of hearing. The head office is at 7-11 Armstrong Road, London W3 7JL.

British Red Cross Society
Check your local telephone directory or write to the Society at 9 Grosvenor Crescent, London SW1X 7EJ. It can arrange to lend such equipment as bedrests, bedpans and waterproof sheets, sometimes such items as wheelchairs, and it also produces useful booklets on caring for someone who is bedridden. Local officials will give valuable direct advice if you are nursing a parent at home and can often provide volunteers to visit, transport and offer other help. You could also try the St John Ambulance Association or the St Andrew's Ambulance Association if you have one locally.

CHARITIES
There are many charities which have funds to help old people, and the local Age Concern branch will know what they are and how to get in touch with them. It may also be

possible to get help from a parent's former place of work,
or that of a deceased spouse, by writing to the personnel
officer. The British Legion, too, could put an ex-
serviceman or servicewoman in touch with a local repre-
sentative of the Forces Help Society, which has a full list
of all the various regimental funds available.

The *Charities Digest*, mentioned several times in this
book, is published by the Family Welfare Association,
501–505 Kingsland Road, London E8 4AU.

Chest, Heart and Stroke Association
The Association publishes informative booklets, books
and leaflets on chest, heart and stroke illnesses. It spon-
sors the Volunteer Stroke Scheme to help in the rehabi-
litation of patients suffering from speech impairment and
supports stroke clubs which aim to aid the social rehabi-
litation of stroke victims. It advises patients on personal
problems that may arise from their illnesses, and can in
certain cases, through social services departments, make
grants to individuals to help with fuel bills, rent and rates
arrears, visits to hospitals and holiday costs. Write to the
Chest, Heart and Stroke Association, Tavistock House
North, Tavistock Square, London WC1H 9JE.

The Council for Voluntary (or Social) Service and the Rural Community Council
The main work of the Councils in their areas is to
co-ordinate all the local voluntary organizations and
advise on which can best help with problems. Sometimes
they produce a directory of organizations, and they can
also tell potential volunteers in which of them they would
be likely to be of most use.

Counsel and Care for the Elderly
This organization too will give help and advice on any
problems to do with elderly people. The case workers
liaise with the statutory services, charities and benevolent
organizations to provide professional advice and grants
towards the costs of nursing care. Write to 131 Middlesex
Street, London E1 7JF.

Cruse

This is the National Organization for the Widowed and Their Children, offering emotional and practical help to widows and widowers wherever they live, whatever their age, nationality or belief. There are over 100 local branches in Britain and a national membership for those beyond the reach of a branch. If your parent has lost a spouse you may find it helpful to obtain a copy of the organization's booklet *Helping the Widowed* and its publications list of over 40 leaflets and fact sheets. Write to Cruse House, 126 Sheen Road, Richmond, Surrey TW9 1UR.

Disabled Living Foundation

This organization has a vast store of information on ways to resolve the daily living problems experienced by disabled elderly people. For example, it can advise on aids and equipment, offer details of the suppliers of special clothes made from easy-care fibres and with easy-to-handle fastenings, and suggest ways of resolving or reducing incontinence or visual-handicap problems. These are just a few examples. Write to, or ring, the Foundation for literature and details of its services at 380–384 Harrow Road, London, W9 2HU (tel: 01–289 6111).

Help the Aged

This national charity is dedicated to improving the quality of life of elderly people in need of help, in the UK and overseas. It pursues this aim by raising and granting funds towards community-based projects, housing and overseas aid. It has its own education department and publishes training and educational material for people of all ages as well as a monthly national newspaper for older people. For further information about its many activities and publications, write to Help the Aged at St James's Walk, London EC1R 0BE.

Hospice movement

This movement, which is becoming widespread throughout the UK, exists to help the terminally ill and their relatives, either in the home or in a hospice, where the patient is cared for and helped to die with dignity and with as little pain as possible. For details, write to St Christopher's Hospice, Lawrie Park Road, Sydenham, London SE26.

Lions International
There are very many local branches of this organization which hold fund-raising events and operate a great number of services and schemes for handicapped and old people. Obtain the address of your nearest Lions branch from your local telephone directory.

Marie Curie Memorial Foundation
The Foundation provides nursing care and support for cancer patients and their families, free of charge. It has eleven residential Marie Curie homes throughout the UK; 4,000 Marie Curie nurses to care for patients in their own homes; cancer education and training for doctors and nurses; and a research institute to improve treatment and help to find a cure. For further information, write to MCMF, 28 Belgrave Square, London SW1X 8QG.

The National Society for Cancer Relief, the address of which is Anchor House, 15–19 Britten Street, London SW3 3TY, could also be contacted. And there are many local organizations or branches of national organizations which can help – check with your local Age Concern office or CAB.

National Association for Mental Health (MIND)
You will naturally discuss any mental or psychological problems that arise in your parent with his or her doctor, but this organization can provide back-up support, advice and help of many kinds. Write to 22 Harley Street, London W1 2ED.

The National Federation of Retirement Associations and The British Pensioners' and Trades Union Association Committee
These organizations campaign for the payment of an adequate pension and the abolition of the Earnings Rule; for better standards of geriatric care; for the provision of

services to alleviate loneliness; and increased opportunities for educational and leisure activities. For local addresses write to the BPTUA at its Head Office, Norman Dodds House, 315 Bexley Road, Erith, Kent DA8 3EZ.

Parkinson's Disease Society
This society exists to help sufferers and their families with advice and guidance on the best way of coping with the condition. It also finances research and disseminates information both from its headquarters and via local branches. The address is 36 Portland Place, London W1N 3DG.

The Pre-Retirement Association
A very useful organization for those soon to retire, it has several affiliated local organizations around the UK. It runs an advice and information service and produces a publications list. Write to the Association at 19 Undine Street, Tooting, London SW17 8PP (enclosing an s.a.e.). Its excellent, very upbeat monthly magazine, *Choice*, is aimed at helping readers to make the most of retirement and is available either from your local newsagent or by subscription to members of the Association.

Religious organizations
Local churches, chapels, synagogues and so on offer much in the way of practical support and visiting, and it is as well to remember that for many old people, as well as their carers, religious beliefs as well as spiritual guidance can be a major source of strength at difficult times. A visit from a priest, minister or other spiritual leader will be a great comfort at a time when the elderly believer's thoughts are inevitably turning towards the time of his or her death.

The Royal National Institute for the Blind
This organization runs braille and tape services, homes, hotels, the Talking Book library and sells specially designed and adapted goods. Also contact the RNIB for advice on welfare and leisure activities and for information leaflets. Write to 224 Great Portland Street, London W1N 6AA.

The Royal National Institute for the Deaf
The Institute exists to carry out research and offer advice and information on all aspects of deafness. The address is 105 Gower Street, London WC1E 6AH.

Women's Royal Voluntary Service
The WRVS organizes the Meals-on-wheels and Books-on-wheels services in many areas and has a network of volunteers who will visit. Services in different parts of the UK vary, but running luncheon clubs, day centres and social clubs for old people, arranging holidays, providing sheltered housing and nursing homes are among the WRVS's many activities. Some branches can provide bedding and clothes for old people, so if you have any you do not want, it might be worth enquiring whether your local WRVS would like to have them.

ACCOMMODATION FOR THE ELDERLY
For lists of residential homes and nursing homes, and of hotels and guest houses which welcome elderly people, contact GRACE (see page 64), PO Box 71, Cobham, Surrey KT11 2HW,

Elderly Accommodation Counsel (see page 67): for a questionnaire, send to 1 Durward House, 31 Kensington Court, London W8 5BH.

Salvation Army For information about Eventide Homes (see page 67), write to Salvation Army at 280 Mare Street, London E8 1HE.

EASY COOKING FOR ELDERLY PEOPLE
Easy Cooking for One or Two by Louise Davies (Penguin) or an excellent free booklet *Healthy Eating in Later Life* (obtainable by sending an s.a.e. not less than 9 × 6 inches to Dulcolax Healthy Eating Offer, Bury House, 126–128 Cromwell Road, London SW7 4ET) are two highly recommended sources of recipes for simple meals that elderly people will enjoy.

Index

Meals-on-wheels 28, 46, 56, 66, 92, 134, 205, 221
medical check-ups 149; services 207-12 *et passim*
medicines 98-102, 112, 121, 146, 158, 164, 179, 181, 184, 198
memory loss 57, 186, 193-6
mental illness 20, 22, 53-4, 65, 67, 172-96, 208, 219
Menuhin, Yehudi 119
MIND 219
mobile homes (caravans) 74, 156
mobility allowance 133-4
moles 169
muggings 182
music 119

national savings certificates 135
neglect (by old person, of self and home) 183-4
nursing the old 171, 197-8, 206, 209-10, 221

obesity 149, 151, 160-1
obsession 183
oil heaters 78
occupational therapist 102, 207, 210
osteopaths 211

parentsitters 91
Parkinson's disease 167-8; Society 220
Pen Friends Club 36
pensions and allowances 127, 128, 130, 131, 132, 219-20
persecution 183
personality changes 21, 44, 145, 175, 202
pets 52-3
physiotherapy/ists 165, 166, 211
piles (haemorrhoids) 160
pneumonia 151
powers of attorney 32, 59, 140-1
premium savings bonds 137
Pre-Retirement Association 25, 220
professional organizations 205
prostate trouble 164, 165
psychiatrists 181, 211-12

radio *see* television and radio
receivership 213
Red Cross *see* British Red Cross Society
registering a death 199
relationships in family 75, 79
relaxation 112
religious bodies 67-8, 81, 172, 199, 220
residential homes *see* homes for the elderly
residential hotels 64-5, 67
rest homes *see* homes for the elderly
retirement 25, 27, 128, 131, 138, 180, 219-20
retirement area, choice of 27
Retirement Associations, National Federation of 219
rheumatism 101, 162, 164, 178
role reversal 59, 117
room temperature 78, 154

Rural Community Council 217

safety 26, 27, 43, 49, 77-8, 102, 105, 156, 189, 202, 213
Salvation Army 67, 201, 221
savings and investments 136-7
sciatica 211
Scottish Home and Health Department 134, 206
security 105, 174, 182, 191
senility *see* confusion *and* dementia
sex 19
sheltered housing 30, 60, 62-4, 68-9
sleep 112, 149, 169, 178-9, 180
slimming 161
smoking 150, 169
social services 24, 29-30, 42, 46, 54, 62, 67, 77, 152, 154, 166, 172, 187, 190, 205-6 *et passim*
solid fuel 42, 78, 155, 157, 176
speech impairment 217
St Andrew's Ambulance Association 216
St John's Ambulance Association 16, 216
stress: in carer 11, 110-19, 172, 178, 185-6, 190, 197, 201; in old person 21
strokes 147-9, 151, 164, 165, 166, 173, 217
suicide 180, 184, 197
swimming 161

'talking books' 151, 220
tax 10, 36, 69, 125-6, 131, 136, 137-9
teeth 103, 128
telephone 41, 53-4, 123-4, 126, 134, 175; for deaf 158, 205
television and radio 54-5, 77, 119, 126, 134, 157, 176, 177, 179, 205
Trade, Department of 213
transport 11, 43, 46, 62, 132, 134, 172, 205, 207, 214

ulcers 179, 170

varicose veins 162
ventilatin 156, 176
villages for the old 72
voluntary organizations 34-7, 43, 46, 52, 62, 66, 67, 84, 88, 91, 170, 181, 203, 214-16, 217
Voluntary (or Social) Service, Council for 214, 217

wandering 57, 120, 174, 189-90
weight loss 180, 201
widow/widower 41, 42 *et passim; see also* Cruse
widows' allowances 132-3
wills 139
women's disorders 162-3
Women's Institute 25, 27
Women's Royal Voluntary Service 214, 221
worry, excessive 181-3
WRVS *see* Women's Royal Voluntary Service